D1010358

OFF TRACK PLANET'S

TRAVEL GUIDE TO

'MERICA!

----------- *for the* -----------

YOUNG, SEXY,
=*and*= BROKE

BY THE EDITORS OF OTP

FREDDIE PIKOVSKY *and* ANNA STAROSTINETSKAYA

RUNNING PRESS
PHILADELPHIA · LONDON

© 2016 by Off Track Planet
Published by Running Press,
A Member of the Perseus Books Group

Books published by Running Press are available at special discounts for bulk purchases in the United States
by corporations, institutions, and other organizations. For more information, please contact
the Special Markets Department at the Perseus Books Group, 2300 Chestnut Street, Suite 200,
Philadelphia, PA 19103, or call (800) 810-4145, ext. 5000, or e-mail special.markets@perseusbooks.com.

ISBN 978-0-7624-5926-1
Library of Congress Control Number: 2015954072

E-book ISBN 978-0-7624-5929-2

9   8   7   6   5   4   3   2   1
Digit on the right indicates the number of this printing

Cover design by Susan Van Horn
Interior design and maps by Corinda Cook
Edited by Jordana Tusman
Typography: Neutraface, Archer, Bebas, Korolev, Roboto, Prohibition, and Wisdom Script

Running Press Book Publishers
2300 Chestnut Street
Philadelphia, PA 19103-4371

Visit us on the web!
www.runningpress.com

CONTENTS

INTRODUCTION

This book is a collection of American places, people, and parts, collaged together to paint a picture of the crazy, resourceful, fun, and sometimes wildly contradictory culture that comprises 'Merica. America is full of exhilarating adventures, from the Adirondacks to the Grand Canyon to the wonders of Yellowstone. This sprawling country's food scene includes everything from artisanal, grass-fed, coddled Michelin-starred cuisine to abominations like tater tot casseroles and State Fair fried butter sticks. And we Americans are quirky

people, some of us making huge sculptures out of car parts in the middle of nowhere.

We dug into the history of this fascinating place, hopping along Route 66 to get a taste of 'Merica's roadside attractions and drinking all the drinks from Kentucky's famed bourbon to Denver's delicious beer. We put this book together as both insiders and observers of this ridiculously entertaining place, jamming the random pieces of America the country together in order to distill 'Merica the culture. Here's how to get the most from this book.

HOW THIS BOOK IS ORGANIZED

This book is divided into regions, including the South, the Yankees (the Northeast), Middle 'Merica, Nebraska and the Like, and the Goddamn Hippies (or the West). The borders can be blurry between territories, and sometimes state lines and cultural qualities don't quite align—like what the hell are Miami and Austin doing in the South?—but such is 'Merica.

You'll find that each region is further organized by interest, including Adventure, Art and Design, Fashion, Food, Music, and Sex and Partying. We take on the Great Lakes, tackle the surprisingly awesome surf spots of the Eastern Seaboard, feast on the soul food of the South, peruse the Rock and Roll Hall of Fame, show you how to woo a Midwesterner, and drink at the West's best swinging-door saloons. Flip to whatever area interests you most,

or read the book cover to cover if you're an overachiever.

Our approach is a little schizophrenic; we jump from modern-day festivals to bro bars, then pull a *Back to the Future* to uncover interesting historical happenings that led to cultural innovations. Sometimes we focus on individuals; other times, we describe larger movements or ideas.

You can use this book as a road trip companion, but not in the traditional sense. We're not mapping out specific routes for you because—Internet. What we do offer is the funnest, most interesting tidbits about 'Merica we could find. This is by no means an exhaustive look at all the cultural quirks 'Merica has to offer. Undoubtedly, there are many small-town wonders left to cover across this land of the free and home of the brave.

A VERY BRIEF HISTORY

Many will argue that American culture is the lack of culture altogether, which is partially true. But the intersections of the many cultures that live side by side create a mega culture that continues to evolve, sometimes from conflict, other times from accepting that coexisting is the only way either will survive. 'Merica is the kind of thing you want to be mad at; but then it does something adorable, and you just can't.

The land between Canada and Mexico was once inhabited by tribes, "Native Americans" or "Indians," as Columbus called them when he "discovered" America in 1492, thinking it was India. This "New World" had promise of a new life and European settlers came to claim various territories for themselves. This part sucks, but it must be said: Slaves from Africa were forced to develop the land, especially in the South, so their masters could prosper.

In 1607, people were sick of Britain's stale scones, so they jumped on the *Mayflower* and parked it in Jamestown, Virginia. Others followed suit, and after issuing a big "Fuck you, Britain," by kicking their ass in

the Revolutionary War from 1775–1783, the first thirteen colonies were formed along the East Coast. New Americans declared their independence from Britain in a formal document in 1776. George Washington became president and the states agreed on a set of ruling principles (aka the Constitution) in 1788.

When all the *i*'s were dotted and the *t*'s crossed, everyone sat around drinking liquor, wondering what else was out there. They decided to expand westward on the claim that it was God's will, or Manifest Destiny, to do so. By 1912, the settlers reached Arizona and gobbled up as much (Native American) land as possible; they also purchased the Louisiana territory from the French in 1803 and put Texas in their pocket after winning the Mexican-American war in 1848. The need for faster transport sparked the building of railroads. Plus, there was gold in California, so faster transport meant more cash money.

As the country expanded, beliefs about how to run shit became discordant with the South, which wanted to hold onto

older traditions (like slaves) and threatened secession from the Union, while the North wanted to move forward as a unified nation. The Civil War lasted from 1861 until 1865, and we're not sure everyone in the South got the memo that it ever ended.

Let's talk about Abe Lincoln for a minute. During this time the country was torn; agriculture down South was built on the backs of slaves, while Northern states instead switched to cheap immigrant labor. Harriet Beecher Stowe, author of the antislavery book *Uncle Tom's Cabin*, gave people literary ammunition to abolish slavery. In 1863, when shit was at its worst, Abe Lincoln issued the Emancipation Proclamation, which was ideally supposed to set all the slaves in the Confederate states free, but newly freed slaves struggled to gain true equality.

Prohibition in the 1920s had a profound effect on the country, splitting it further into super-sober Prohibitionists and bootleggers. By 1933, the drunks won the fight, and things like NASCAR and Kentucky bourbon became part of 'Merica's drunk culture. Sparked by the stock market crash of 1929, the Great Depression threw the world into a broke-ass economic tailspin. Franklin D. Roosevelt put together the New Deal to help America recover, which included government assistance programs, safety nets for the elderly, and other social services.

The surprise attack by the Japanese at Pearl Harbor in 1941 got America into

I WANT YOU
FOR U.S.ARMY
NEAREST RECRUITING STATION

Loves to go...*and looks it !*

The '56 Chevrolet

The Bel Air Sport Sedan is one of two new Chevrolet 4-door hardtops. All 19 new models feature Body by Fisher.

It's got frisky new power . . . V8 or 6 . . . to make the going sweeter and the passing safer. It's agile . . . quick . . . solid and sure on the road!

This, you remember, is the car that set a new record for the Pikes Peak run. And the car that can take that tough and twisting climb in record time is bound to make your driving safer and more fun.

Curve ahead? You level through it with a wonderful nailed-to-the-road feeling of stability. Chevrolet's special suspension and springing see to that.

Slow car ahead? You whisk around it and back in line in seconds. Chevrolet's new high-compression power—ranging

from the new "Blue-Flame 140" Six up to 225 h.p. in the new Corvette V8 engine, available at extra cost—handles that.

Quick stop called for? Nudge those oversize brakes and relax. Chevrolet's exclusive Anti-Dive braking brings you to a smooth, *heads-up* halt.

No doubt about it, this bold beauty was made for the road. Like to try it? Just see your Chevrolet dealer. . . . Chevrolet Division of General Motors, Detroit 2, Michigan.

CHEVROLET

World War II to fight against Japan and Germany on the Allied side. The United States became the "arsenal of democracy," producing weapons for war that, in turn, meant everyone had jobs. Postwar America was back on its feet and the '50s brought an era of innovation. Roads sprawled from sea to shining sea, suburbia was born, motorist culture began, and roadside advertisements, motels, and fast food boomed. 'Merica was a culture of planned obsolescence, and disposable incomes were spent on newer and better things.

While the United States was tangentially involved in the war in Vietnam since 1949, the escalation of American troops that flooded into Vietnam between 1961 and '62 set off a counterculture of students and other young people who did everything to avoid recruitment into a war they didn't support. While the government put out Commie blacklists, the hippies in the West preached peace and love. Concurrently, the civil rights movement, led by Martin

Luther King Jr., was in full swing and people were determined to fight for the equal rights promised by Abe Lincoln.

The carefree disco days of the '70s saw the rise of both drugs and AIDS. When AIDS spread like wildfire, being gay was not okay. It wasn't until the turn of the twenty-first century that people finally began accepting AIDS as an everyone disease and not just something you got from having homosexual thoughts. What happened in the '80s? Big hair and shoulder pads, mostly.

The '90s under Clinton were full of shenanigans (ahem, Monica) and Dubya continues to be the butt of many a joke. In 2009, Obama made history as the first black president to take office.

For decades, the hot topic in any governmental debate has been immigration, which hits 'Merica in the heart. This land was made for you and me—and America's been working on making that true since Columbus sailed the ocean blue.

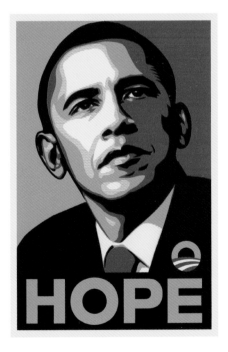

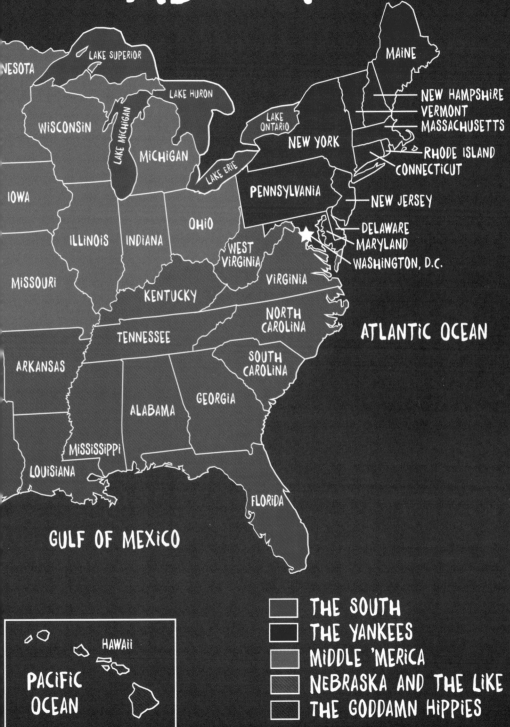

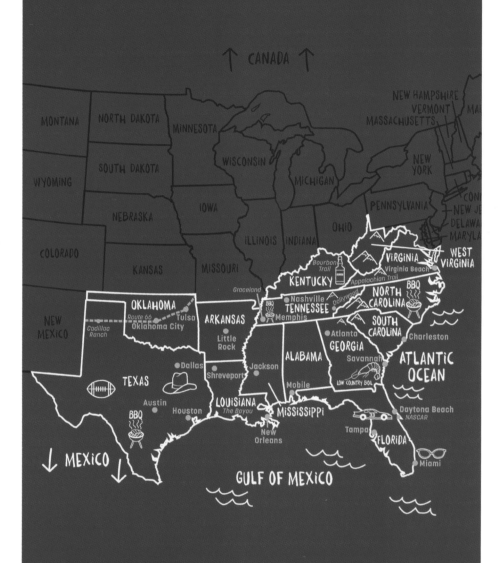

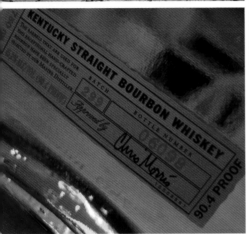

THE SOUTH

At once a place of pride and shame, the South has spawned many a stereotype, and some of them still hold true. Here, people love their guns, bacon, and Republican politics. The birthplace of country, jazz, blues, and BBQ, the South is a place of good manners, where charm trumps all. Not everything fits neatly into the South geographically, with Miami out doing its own crazy thing and Austin keeping things weird. Get tipsy on the Bourbon Trail, visit a megachurch, and don't forget to scream "NASCAR!" at the top of your lungs.

FIVE MUST-HAVE APPALACHIAN ADVENTURES

The scenic connection between the North and the Southeast, the Appalachian Trail isn't a day-trip trek. This thing will bring out your inner beast with each of its five million steps. A 2,175-mile journey from Georgia to Maine, through North Carolina, Tennessee, Virginia, West Virginia, Maryland, Pennsylvania, New Jersey, New York, Connecticut, Massachusetts, Vermont, and New Hampshire, the trail crosses five national parks and incredible mountain ranges, with campsites set up along the way to rest your adventurous soul. These five must-have adventures really squeeze the most out of this vast and varied terrain.

THE LINVILLE GORGE

Getting smacked around in foamy white water is about as thrilling as it gets. The rushing Linville Gorge is ideal for whitewater rafting and drops more than the beat on Saturday night, throwing you into the liquid abyss. It starts at Babel Tower and ends at Conley Cove, and while it's only 3.8 miles long, it's a solid Class V the whole way through. People often exaggerate its length because it takes about six hours to complete and none of them want to admit they were moving at a snail's pace. There's no shame in the game here; this thing is tough.

WATERFALL CAMPING

The Smoky Mountains, named for their distinctive fog caps, lie on the border of Tennessee and North Carolina. Getting

into the Smokies, you'll have access to the park's insane hiking trails, some of which will take you into the spray of its many waterfalls. You can walk behind the Grotto, watch the cascading falls of the rushing Ramsey Cascades, and hike up to the chimney tops for 360-degree views. You can set up camp in the backcountry near Mount LeConte and watch a spectacular sunset at Myrtle Point. Wildflowers and bears are abundant.

OTP Tip: Although it sounds super-shoddy, the Craggy Gardens are a spectacle of fairy-tale wonder you must experience on foot.

> ===== *Fun Fact* =====
>
> Ruby Falls in Tennessee is the deepest underground waterfall in all the land.

GET TO THE TOP: CLINGMANS DOME

Clingmans Dome, with an observation tower that looks like a flying saucer, is the highest point in the Smokies and Tennessee. The weather runs cool during the winter, when the trees get all iced over, but the trails are closed then, which means you'll have to ski in. From the top, you'll see spruce and fir forests and, when the weather's right, the short, steep hikes are a challenging way to get around.

HANG-GLIDE AT LOOKOUT MOUNTAIN

Along the Cumberland Plateau, between Georgia and Tennessee, you can try your hand at defying gravity by hang-gliding around like a bird catching wind. The conditions for gliding here are ideal and, on

most days, you only need to run three to four steps off the ridge before you're airborne. The mountains are broad, and flying above them feels like swimming in a sea of sky. The park employees will hold your hand (more like spoon you from behind), if you're a novice pilot, with training sessions. Tandem flights and all equipment, including some awesome gliders, are available for sale if you're the Chuck Norris of hang-gliding.

> ===== *Fun Fact* =====
>
> Check out the abandoned launch-pad in Highfield-Cascade, Maryland, created by flight enthusiasts and deemed too dangerous to launch from. People come here to contemplate and tag the shit out of the ridge.

F*CK IT,
HIKE THE WHOLE THING!

The Appalachian Trail is long, rocky, and rough, but it was meant to be hiked, and hike it you must. If you're looking to set some endurance records and know what you're doing out in the wilderness, hiking the entire trail will be a long, arduous, unforgettable journey that about twelve thousand people have done since its completion in 1937. It takes five to seven months, the optimal start time is mid- to late spring, people go mostly south to north, and the midway point is Harpers Ferry, West Virginia.

Towns are four to five days apart so this will either be super-exciting to you or you'll die of starvation. The trail was built for "thru-hikers," so you can leave the tent at home because there are strategically placed shelters about eight miles apart. You'll have to dig a hole to poop in (although some shelters have toilets). If you're the overly ambitious type, you can do a round-trip, but then you'll have to write a book about it.

THE BOURBON TRAIL

Shot for shot, Kentucky is the holy land of bourbon. Sippin' on the stuff is good and dandy, but you don't know BO until you've staggered along the Bourbon Trail. Grab your bike and line your gut with steel; we're setting off on a tour of the best brown liquid 'Merica has to offer.

AMERICA'S NATIVE SPIRIT

Evan Williams opened the first distillery in 1783 along the Ohio River in Louisville. Shortly thereafter, lots of folks tried their hand at deepening the flavor of plain ol' whiskey by aging it in barrels. Eventually, booze-lovers settled in Louisville, Bardstown, and Frankfort to brew their bourbon tax-free. Kentucky was just a wee baby then and only officially became a state in 1792, with Bourbon County established in 1785. Officially named "bourbon" in 1840, it became America's national spirit by 1964 and rules for what can be classified as bourbon were established.

WHAT'S THE BIG DEAL?

Corn's the big deal. Corn is native to 'Merica and therefore distinguishes this particular type of whiskey from similar booze, like scotch from Scotland. The mixture must be 51 percent corn to be considered bourbon and the rest is made up from a proprietary blend of grains. The mash mixture must be aged in charred new oak barrels, and to be called "straight bourbon," it must be aged for a minimum of two years. Kentuckians are convinced that their water is the best (due to its low iron content) and they swear it contributes to the taste of the final product. Bourbon-making takes patience, a process that fits with the slow pace of life in this part of the South.

> ===== *Fun Fact* =====
>
> *Sour mash* is a fermentation process similar to sourdough bread making, where yeast is added to the by-products of whiskey production as a fermentation agent. This mixture is then added to new batches of whiskey to sour them, creating a complex flavor profile as it ages.

PACK THE TRAIL MIX

An expansive area of land that has been busy with bourbon since the beginnings of 'Merica, the best way to go is by motorcycle or bike. The trail is full of gorgeous green rolling hills, and the main attraction is hanging out and learning about bourbon from proud Kentuckians. This isn't like Vegas, where you stumble from place to place because some distilleries are up to seventy miles apart; it *is* like Disneyland, though, with lots of interactive experiences.

Cost at the distilleries varies from $5 to $40, and the tours are about an hour and a half each. Unless you plan to make drinking bourbon a full-time job for a day, bet on staying in Kentucky for three to four days, if only to sleep off the bourbon brain. There are a total of nine distilleries and if you pick up a "passport" at the visitor's center and hit them all, you'll get a free T-shirt! Here's a sampling of what you'll find.

Heaven Hill Distillery

This distillery is a must-hit for history. Elijah Craig, a traveling Baptist preacher and entrepreneur, is known to some as the inventor of bourbon, but so many distillers were making the spirit at the same time in the same way that it's hard to give him all the credit. That's not to say that Elijah's firewater, found at Heaven Hill, isn't some of the best in the world. But Craig's isn't the only attraction here.

Pappy Van Winkle began producing his Old Rip Van Winkle bourbon right before Prohibition at the now shuttered Stitzel Weller distillery, and no dumb federal law was going to stop the old dude (who kept making the good juice until he was eighty-nine). His distillery had a "medicinal whiskey" license, much like cannabis dispensaries in California in the dark days of weed. When the place was shuttered, the bottles were distributed to Buffalo Trace (off the trail in Frankfort) and Heaven Hill distilleries.

Woodford Reserve

You can't have Jack Daniel's on the Kentucky Bourbon Trail because it's in

Tennessee and they call it "Tennessee whiskey." They refuse to call it bourbon because they claim the distinguishing use of charcoal filtering sets their drink apart. Truth is, Woodford Reserve Distillery also puts its famous bourbon through a charcoal filter, so, really, Tennesseeans don't know Jack, and the stuff here tastes quite similar.

Fun Fact

In 2013, a few idiots were busted for stealing seven to eight thousand cases of Pappy Van Winkle. They were also into sexting and bragging about how much money they were making.

Four Roses

This stuff is just plain ol' delicious. We won't bore you with more history, but Four Roses is aged in a single-story rack warehouse that the distillers claim is responsible for its subtle flavor.

More breath-souring bourbon can be found at Four Roses, Evan Williams, Wild Turkey, Town Branch, Maker's Mark, Samuels, and your old college dorm best friend, Jim Beam. Many distilleries shut down during the hotter summer months, so do the trail in September when you'll get full tours, and be there to honor National Bourbon Heritage Month.

DO THE DERBY RIGHT

Kentucky is known for three things: bourbon, chicken, and the derby. While a deep understanding of horse racing isn't necessary to do the derby right, the factors below are absolutely crucial to getting the most out of the race.

HATS OFF

Big, obnoxious hats are a must. The bigger, more decked out in flowers and ribbons, the better. Back in 1875, the derby's creator wanted to shift the perception of gamblin' on horses from a low-life activity to a high-fashion event. He stuck his wife and her friends in a wagon and used their flashy hats to gain attention from the kind of people that liked (and could afford) big flashy hats. These days, the hats steal the show.

MINT JULEPS

Served in a silver cup, this bourbon and mint drink has been the official beverage of the derby (and any hot day in Kentucky) since 1938. If your horse wins, consider blowing your earnings on a $1,000 julep, served in a gold cup with a silver straw.

BIG BETTING

There are thirteen races and twenty horses running on Derby Day. Pick your race (or the whole derby) and your favorite horse and walk up to the window with cash. Depending on how sure you are about your stallion, you can put money down on the horse winning an individual race, the whole derby, or "across" the finish line (which means if your horse places first, second, or third, you'll be rolling in dough).

"RUN FOR THE ROSES"

When you're good and sloshed, your big hat slouching somewhere between your neck and your ankles, you'll be reminded that you're at a horse race by the bright red garland being draped onto the winning horse. This is when you check your ticket to see if you're a millionaire.

NASCAR: 'MERICA'S FIRST DRUNK DRIVERS

NASCAR would never be the glorious, somewhat backward, spectacle it is without hooch. Stock cars were souped up in order to transport booze better and faster during Prohibition, and legend has it that when the dudes would drive their moonshine around, they'd race on the back roads, because why not? Bootleggers would outsmart and outdrive the law all the while getting in some good racing practice, with quick delivery on the hooch. Eventually, it became better organized, with crude tracks laid down to see who the fastest "runner" was. Bill France Sr. stepped in to put the rules down in Daytona Beach, Florida, and in 1947, the National Association for Stock Car Auto Racing (NASCAR!) was born, with Big Bill at the wheel.

NASCAR?

NASCAR is basically a repository for displays of Southern masculinity, like the WWE, but with dangerous vehicles and high speeds, instead of spandex and fake head butts. And, fortunately, nobody really cares that deeply about NASCAR outside of the South. The spectacle is the aggression, "settling the score" story lines between races. If you're going to go all NASCAR on people, you'll want to know the key players and facts:

🏁 The Darlington Raceway in South Carolina was the first official track.

🏁 The Daytona 500 Sprint Cup Series is the super bowl of NASCAR. Same kind of drunks; different kind of game.

🏁 Junior Johnson (aka the "Last American Hero") spent time in the Ohio slammer for operating a moonshine still, but then went right back to racing, winning fifty races before retiring in 1966. What's old Johnson up to now? He owns a NASCAR racing team, makes pork products, and sells "Midnight Moon Moonshine."

🏁 Lee Petty won the first ever race at the Daytona International Speedway by bitching his way to the top. Johnny Beauchamp was declared the unofficial winner when they came

nose-to-nose at the finish line, but Petty refused to lose, and after three days of deliberation, he was named the winner. Persistence pays, kids!

🏁🏁 Richard Petty is Lee's son, and was a total disaster at first. Nonetheless, he became a legend and earned his nickname, "The King" (move over Elvis), by winning the NASCAR Championship seven times, with a number of top finishing records under his belt during his long career. Petty retired in 1992 when hot young studs like Dale Earnhardt Jr. and Jeff Gordon started burning up the track.

NASCAR!

Is NASCAR less prestigious than most other races that happen around the world? Formula One, for instance? Heck, yes, it is, but this is NASCAR! And it's all-American. What's the fun, you ask, in watching someone continuously turn left? It's all in the fans. NASCAR is a very easy "sport" to understand: The first car across the finish line wins; this works as a bonding agent. More importantly, people get behind drivers' personas, and that's where the real fan base is built. Plus, crashes happen all the time and it creates a bit of a hockey brawl

mentality as far as the fans are concerned, but that fear of risk, death, and destruction is the very thing that keeps it all exciting.

NASCAR's safety rules are far more relaxed than Formula One's, which require drivers to wear neck braces. But this is 'Merica! and we do shit that's dangerous and explosive. Dale Earnhardt's skull fracture death made NASCAR officials pause a bit, but not enough to institute real safety regulations. "Generation Five" race cars were introduced in 2007, where the car bodies were wrapped uniformly (regardless of the maker's design features) for safety purposes. But big car companies didn't like this, so by 2013, "Generation Six" cars were born, which reverted back to letting carmakers show off brands with more pizzazz, regardless of safety concerns.

NASCAR!!

Is it all *Talladega Nights*? We'd say the film painted a pretty accurate picture. Confederate flags will fly high and God will be mentioned at every turn. It is a sport that embodies the far right, and rivalries, driving, drinking, and babes are all part of the action. NASCAR!

ART and DESIGN

CADILLAC RANCH

Out in the distance of a dusty road, illuminated by the orange, nay, yellow, Amarillo, Texas, sun sits a majestic art installation composed of ten Cadillacs, nosedown in the ground, tail fins pointing toward the sky. Bruce Springsteen wrote a song about it, Disney's *Cars* used it as symbolic background, and many have come to pray before the Cadillac gods, and have graffiti-ed them to shit in the name of self-expression. But these ten Caddies aren't just there for shock value. Cadillac Ranch captures the life—and death—of the American Dream.

CADDY CONCEPT

Cadillac Ranch was conceived by art collective Ant Farm in a San Francisco bar in the 1970s. The duo found a children's book called *The Look of Cars*, which sparked nostalgia for the Caddy era in their hearts, inspiring them to look to a rich old dude, wacky oil billionaire Stanley Marsh 3, to fund a grand-scale project to memorialize their fond memories. In 1974, Marsh's Amarillo, Texas, property became the "hood ornament of Route 66."

SPECS

Ant Farm set out to realize their vision by digging through junkyards for Caddies that fit the bill. Once the ten Caddies were acquired, for an average of $200 a pop, they drove or dropped the cars, nose-down, into pre-dug, eight-foot holes on Marsh's land, cementing them to match the angle of Egypt's Giza Pyramid. The cars were set up in sequential order by year of make, skipping years when the tail fin wasn't altered much.

Why tail fins? The replacement of piston propliners with jet engines at the beginning of the 1950s propelled America into the "jet age." The modernization of air travel, coupled with the expansion of the interstate, created an obsession with futuristic aesthetics and the open road. Carmakers began designing tiny tail fins, reminiscent of jets, and the trend grew well into the '60s, with fins jetting out sharply from the backsides of new models.

The jet-inspired tail fin represented power and prestige, two things people had forgotten they wanted. Caddy Ranch's ten models are a perfect arc of tail fins, from the tiny nub of the first model, to the sharp, ridiculous fins of the later models. The Ranch is almost a perfect graph of the life lived during this era of excess and exploration. This time shaped the American Dream.

Fun Fact

Stanley Marsh 3 loved his wife Wendy so much that he had the Caddy Ranch painted pink for her birthday one year.

PLANNED OBSOLESCENCE

You've heard *planned obsolescence* applied to 1950s toasters, TVs, and those Blu-ray discs nobody ever got into. Apple is good at this. Turns out, planned obsolescence also applies to cars. The race to the cooler-looking tail fin between Chrysler, GM, and other car manufacturers led to new models being pumped out every year. The older models fell out of fashion and function fast, then ended up at resellers. This meant that, suddenly, people with less money could afford them. The American Dream seemed within reach for the less fortunate, and car-centric businesses, like drive-in restaurants, drive-throughs, and drive-in movies, all meant that you would be seen in and with your car. The expansion of highways and the creation of the interstate system by Eisenhower in '55 (the "open road") also led to an explosion of car sales.

Caddies were synonymous with sexual liberation; more specifically, they meant you no longer needed to bang on your parents' couch. The roadsides sprouted motels and greasy-spoon diners to feed people's appetites for freedom from their homes. Billboards on highways allowed for more ad space, and the Mad Men marketing era boomed.

DEATH OF THE DREAM

The very thing (jets) that led to the popularity of Caddies also led to their demise, as air travel (and foreign importing) became easier and foreign imports more accessible. With globalization on the horizon, German and Japanese cars became "hot" commodities, kicking Caddies into the dust. Rising gas prices and auto dependency meant Americans looked for efficiency over flash. America's needs changed and began to be serviced by foreign brands.

Installed in 1974, the Cadillac Ranch, according to Ant Farm, was "intended to be

both about capturing the American dream and tail fin culture, but also a burial of the gas guzzler." People in Priuses pull off the road to take pictures of the Caddies. Oftentimes, you'll find the cars painted different colors to commemorate events. They were rainbow for gay pride, pink camo for breast cancer awareness, black when a member of Ant Farm died, repainted in their original colors for marketing purposes, and then blanked out with white paint to allow (and encourage) new graffiti to be sprayed on them.

Bruce Springsteen's song is about how Cadillac Ranch is where Caddies go to die, and, well, we all know what happened to the sad characters in the movie *Cars*. But a certain part of 'Merica will always live on in those Caddies, facedown in the dirt between Earth and sky.

ROADSiDE 66

The story of this highway (aka the Mother Road and Main Street of America) is perhaps the single most symbolic representation of how 'Merica came to be. Route 66 was first established in 1926, starting in Chicago and traversing Missouri, Kansas, Oklahoma, Texas, and New Mexico, before ending in Santa Monica, California. It ran continuously for almost 2,500 miles. People took to the road and attractions sprouted up along the route to draw in motorists with the weirdest attention-grabbing shit. This was the beginning of truck stops, fast food, and eventually, when a new interstate, wider roads, and a freeway cut 66 to pieces—ghost towns. While Route 66 lost its highway status in 1985, historic remnants are still hanging by the side of the road. From Chicago to Santa Monica, these are our favorite places still thriving in the name of nostalgia.

ILLINOIS (SPRINGFIELD)

Shea's Gas Station Museum in Springfield used to be a Texaco, but now it houses the coolest gas station memorabilia, like pumps, phone booths, and all kinds of road signs.

> === *Fun Fact* ===
>
> Dixie Truckers Home in McLean is one of the oldest truck stops in America.

MISSOURI (LEBANON)

The neon signs on the Munger Moss Motel have been drawing in weary travelers from the side of the road since Route 66's heyday.

KANSAS (GALENA)

The shortest stretch of the original highway (only thirteen miles) went through Kansas. The former 4 Women on the Route (now Cars on the Route), a service station and rest stop, has now been restored as an attraction dedicated to the movie *Cars*, complete with a big-eyed tow truck.

OTP Tip: The World's Largest Collection of the Smallest Version of the World's Largest Things is a traveling attraction in Lucas, Kansas that contains exactly what you'd expect, given the name.

OKLAHOMA (ARCADIA)

A giant soda ("pop") bottle is a colorful, sixty-six-foot-high structure covered in LED lights that stands in front of POPS soda ranch, a diner that serves six hundred kinds of soda.

TEXAS (AMARILLO)

The seventy-two-ounce Steak Challenge is one of the oldest Route 66 gimmicks, with its "Eat it in an hour and it's free" motto that continues to draw hungry, cheap bastards to Amarillo.

OTP Tip: Keep your eyes on the road between El Paso, Texas, and Tucson, Arizona, where signs like THE THING? MYSTERY OF THE DESERT hype up the attraction in Dragoon, Arizona. After a handful of "Thing" signs, you'll be itching to find out what this damn thing is. So what is the Thing? We're not going to ruin it for you.

ARIZONA (HOLBROOK)

The Wigwam Motel is a collection of teepees and a unique draw for motorists who are sick of motels and want to switch it up a bit.

CALIFORNIA (SANTA MONICA)

While there's the pier and Hotel California (not from the Eagles song, but Santa Monica capitalizes on it anyway), the ocean is the biggest draw here. People keep pedalin' once they see the big blue sea, as it means relief from the road and a new beginning.

THE FIVE SEXIEST SOUTHERN CHURCHES

There's nothing more sinful than sliding down the church pew commando, and these places of worship provide the perfect visual backdrop for such naughtiness. Many churches are built as a symbol of respect to God and these are the sexiest structures to honor the man upstairs.

ANTHONY CHAPEL, HOT SPRINGS, ARKANSAS

Right in the middle of Garvan Woodland Gardens, this chapel is constructed with its lush surroundings in mind. Its six-story-high walls are solid glass, with thin support beams jetting out geometrically like blades of wheat. All that natural light gives everything a sultry glow. Weddings may not be so sexy but if you're going that route, the Anthony Chapel is one of the most popular places to tie the knot in 'Merica.

ST. MARY'S CHURCH OF THE FRESCOES, WEST JEFFERSON, NORTH CAROLINA

If old paintings of men draped in flowy fabrics don't get your Jesus juices flowing, we don't know what will. Painted by a local artist in 1974, the frescoes inside this church are sure to put a notch on your Bible belt. It's a pocket-sized church and will slightly remind you of that great scene from *Kill Bill*.

CATHEDRAL OF ST. JOHN THE BAPTIST, SAVANNAH, GEORGIA

Among the things that take our breath away, gothic architecture, with its swooping arches and pointy rooftops, is right up there with afternoon delights. And this one's French gothic . . . ooh la la. It features a stained-glass interior with an amber-glowing altar and two sky-high spires that were restored after a fire nearly destroyed the church in 1898.

ST. LOUIS CATHEDRAL, NEW ORLEANS, LOUISIANA

Sporting a triple steeple, the St. Louis Cathedral looks a lot like Disneyland. While Goofy is nowhere to be found, this place is sure to conjure up memories of trying to get laid on "It's a Small World." Since its first appearance in the middle of the French Quarter in 1718, the cathedral has undergone extensive renovation and restoration, most recently after Hurricane Katrina. What's sexier than remembering the innocent days of Disney? The church is said to be haunted by two ghosts, whose voices and apparitions can be heard and seen on the grounds. Holy goose bumps!

SECOND BAPTIST CHURCH, HOUSTON, TEXAS

If you're only interested in size, the grand opera house facilities at this Houston megachurch really stand up to the "bigger is better" Texas motto. This house of worship has three larger-than-life big screens, an enormous pipe organ, and enough seating to accommodate 22,000 churchgoers weekly. You like it big and rich? This thing has an annual budget of $55 million.

OTP Tip: If bigger than big is better, the Lakewood Church, also in Houston, is basically a football stadium (with room for over 43,000 attendees) and *New York Times* best seller and touring pastor Joel Osteen broadcasts his sermons from there to over one hundred countries monthly.

WTF ARE WHIRLIGIGS?

In North Carolina, the land of war memorials, something previously called "Acid Park" and possibly dedicated to drugs would be quite refreshing. Whirligigs—or trippy kinetic windmills made of metal scraps, reflective tabs, car parts, and various road signs—used to sit creepily off the side of a road, creaking with the wind and reflecting the light of passing headlights. While the 'gigs have since been moved to less creepy grounds, the myth surrounding their construction survives. Plus, their creator, Vollis Simpson, remains an artistic legend around these parts.

THE MYTH

On prom night, Carol Simpson and her boyfriend did some acid. On the way home, they drove off the road, wrapped the car around a tree, and Carol was killed instantly. The boyfriend, still trippin' hard, went over to the Simpsons' house and told Carol's dad, Vollis Simpson, about what happened, describing his hallucinations. Vollis got to work on Acid Park to re-create what the boyfriend said Carol saw before her death, which was apparently a bunch of trippy windmills.

THE TRUTH

Vollis's daughter is still alive. Vollis was a funny old man who just loved building cool shit. His art was recognized by various local museums, and he was commissioned to build a "gig" for the 1996 Atlanta Olympics. Back in the Acid Park days, the property was closed to the public, but if you promised to shut the fuck up about the LSD, the Simpsons would let you hang out. His explanation for them? He made them to draw the viewer in and delight people.

THE "WHIRLIGIGS"

While the urban legend might be just that, we still think LSD had something to do with it. Anybody who (1) makes shiny windmills in the middle of nowhere, and (2) calls them "whirligigs," has likely done his fair share of acid. During the day, the place looked like a ghost town carnival. The rhythmic crackle of metal parts grinding against each other

at night, illuminated only by specks of light picked up by their reflectors, mimicked the best kind of acid trip. The awe-inspiring haunting gigs sat on Vollis's farm until his death at ninety-four in 2013.

THE NEW GIG

Eventually, the whirligigs began deteriorating; the colors were fading and the metal scraps were rusting, and Vollis knew they would fall into disrepair if he didn't do something to preserve them. Prior to his death, Vollis sold his whirligigs to a project that promised to give them the tender love and care they needed. The Whirligig Park is slated to open in downtown Wilson, North Carolina, with thirty-one of his impressive sculptures serving as a tribute to the beloved local artist, and a performance stage and a lawn to roll around on. The gigs will still be whirling, but not with that same eerie, carny flair. The Whirligig Festival is held every November in Vollis's honor.

Sunday morning church hats are something of a legend down South. In the Bible, the apostle Paul commanded ladies to cover their heads during worship. Southern women took this idea and dressed it up into a statement of feathery, wild-brimmed, colorful glamour and individuality. But these hats are more than just head covers; they represent the triumphant emergence of black women into the public eye in all their holy glory.

HAT-STORY

Called "crowns," church hats were a way for servant women to express themselves in full technicolor, with ribbons, bows, and accoutrements. Putting on a crown on Sunday made each one of them feel like a queen as they stepped out of the drab house clothes they wore during the work-week. As a way to look more formal, the tradition was born to honor God and look good doing it. Hats evolved to serve as status symbols, when newly freed slaves started making salaries and spent their money on new hats and matching accessories, like gloves, purses, and shoes. On Easter and Mother's Day the big hats came out, and collecting them (at $100–$1,000 a pop) became a thing.

VANITY OR RESPECT?

The popularity of wearing wild hats to church made some people question whether women were dressing up for God or just to get attention. While it's a complicated matter, hats are about (hat)titude. You've got to develop a certain level of self-confidence to rock something that looks like a tropical bird on your head. These are "Look at me" hats because their wearers were often treated as second-class citizens. And while sporting them does indeed garner attention, the self-expression element here trumps any claim of narcissism.

RULES OF THE CROWN

Church hats aren't without their rules, however. Some basic tenets are that your hat can't be wider than your shoulders or darker than your shoes. Easter hats are white, cream, or pastel, and veils are a common accessory. Under no circumstances can you touch a lady's hat.

FRINGE BENEFITS

Hat stores and designers popped up to serve the growing demand for new, specialty hats. This was an impetus for black women to open businesses, and people like Mae Reeves opened shops that gained national recognition from celebrities like Ella Fitzgerald. White women were not exempt from the apostle's commandment and had to wear hats, too. This created a point of equality between women when shopping for hats, a way to interact on a level that didn't pit them against each other. For black women, dressing up in hats and matching outfits made them look distinguished and sometimes allowed them to circumvent segregation laws because people treat each other differently when they're fancy-looking.

HATS OFF

New hairstyles in the '70s relegated hats to older generations because Afros and braids didn't fit under crowns as well. The crazy hats are disappearing, but can still be found in many Zionist churches down South, especially on Easter Sunday.

THE LONE STAR STATE LOOK

The Lone Star State look is so identifiable that a misplaced Texan anywhere else sticks out more than a Midwesterner in Manhattan. Every piece is loud, proud, and originally worn to serve a purpose. These days, you don't have to lasso anything to look like you do. While many fringed, suede, and flashy accessories do make for an exceptional faux cowboy, all you really need are a couple of key things. You should probably get a horse because, otherwise, the stuff you're wearing makes no sense.

MANY-GALLON HATS

An umbrella in the rain, shade from the sun, a genius dust blocker—the cowboy hat, with its long, wide brim is the most iconic hat in 'Merica! Utility cowboy hats are made of heavy felt and plainly shaped when first purchased. Over time, the cowboy scrunches it wherever he needs protection from the elements, and his adjustments create folds and bends, which lead to a one-of-a-kind hat style. The Stetson is the most popular hat and many come fashioned with stampede strings, or leather ropes that strap the hat down to your face so it doesn't blow off in the wind.

The ten-gallon cowboy hat evolved from the sombrero and the word *galon* meant "braided hatband," which Mexicans wore as a symbol of status. A hat that could hold ten "galons" would mean the wearer was pretty fucking important, right? And so the cowboy adopted the term, referring to his hat in liquid measures but keeping liquid out of it at all costs (because putting it in there would make for a soggy hat and nobody wants that).

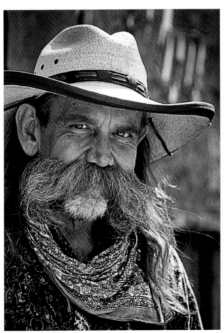

BOOTS WITH THE SPURS

True cowboy boots are high and made of thick bull leather to protect as much of the leg as possible from rubbing. Since they were so stiff, the tops had to have handles so they could be pulled on and removed. They are not walking shoes; they are horse-riding shoes. Comfortable strolls are not the goal here. A narrow toe helps with getting into the stirrup with ease, and heel heights depend on your cowboying activities and are used as a stopper so that foot doesn't slip.

"Roper" boots are shorter, with flatter heels for fast dismounts so you can rope steer, and "stacked" boots feature higher heels for longer rides so your feet stay inside the stirrups. The best boots were made by taking wooden hand-carved molds of people's feet to ensure the perfect snug fit; Lucchese has been making some stylish boots since 1883.

Lone Star ornamentation on the top of boots used to be the jam, and bragging about the battle scars on your boots is common and prideful. Lifting up your hem to show off your boots is a flash of show-offery in cowboy land. What are the spurs for? Why to spook your horse, of course.

BANGIN' BUCKLE BELT

Belts were originally worn loose because your holster was on it and the gun weighed a ton so you didn't want it jammed up into your body. Where did the buckle come from? According to the *Urban Dictionary*, a Texas belt buckle is when you pull your ballsack out over your belt. The thing about Texas is that even when it comes to the simple task of keeping your pants up, if you're not doing it big, you're not doing it right. Their giant man-buckles usually have decorations and inscriptions that either feature "God Bless America" or imprints of a lone star—several of them. It's a billboard, with or without balls on it.

USEFUL ACCESSORIES

You could do well with just a hat, boots, and a buckle, but some delicate bits would run into real danger without a little fashionable protection with flair. Here are five other things you should pick up at the Hootin' Tootin' Cowboy Depot:

1. Chaps (assless or not) protect against cactus thorns and branches, and chaps made out of goat hide with the hair still attached are definitely preferable.

2. A good vest that cradles your dad bod. Think less Richard Simmons and more Clint Eastwood. Since pants and shirts had no pockets back in the day, vests were basically one giant pocket, and we all know how important pockets are.

3. A loose coat so you don't sweat, because once you stop moving, the desert night will make sure all that sweat turns into a deep freeze.

4. Speaking of sweat, a nice, soft bandanna. Civil War soldiers were issued protective neckgear (leather stocks), but it was harsh, so cowboys switched to bandannas to absorb sweat.

5. Anything with fringe. It's made to flutter in the wind, for effect, like hair in a convertible.

Cowboy fashions have been resistant to change due to their highly utilitarian nature. You start making things that don't serve a purpose and they get in the way of ridin' your horse and shootin' up the saloon. Movies represented cowboy fashion as glitzy and glammy. Karl Lagerfeld brought Texas fashion into the mainstream, transforming it into something sparkly and not at all about utility (which likely pissed off many a cowboy). This explains why chicks in California will wear cowboy boots and skirts to festivals without a horse in sight.

LADIES AND GENTS

While people in other regions are into their fashionista experiments, the South has a certain fashion flair that's always weather- and occasion-appropriate. The Southern way of dressing is nuanced, and laced with gender role stereotypes. Regardless, Southerners know how to look damn good.

LADIES

There's a saying that a Southern woman is "strong as oak and sweet as honeysuckle." Looking put together means the world takes you more seriously. Put away your fishnets and sideboob tanks; this is about subtle sexiness.

Hairstyles vary, but volume is king. Since caking on a bunch of makeup in the humid heat is not an option, your skin must be on point. Plus, you must smell like a bouquet of flowers. This beauty regimen will take time, and down in the South, time is what you've got. As for clothes, you'll need to embrace pastels. Sundresses in the summer are crucial and since it's all about femininity, you'll have to get into some underclothes—matching ones. Not that holey bra and those emergency panties.

How do you look like a Southern belle in the heat of summer, but not smell like a hot pile of garbage? It's going to take

some work and an old-school, ornate fan. And no good outfit will give you charm; you've gotta work your social skills and flirt, but nothing raunchy. Manners are part of the outfit and charm schools still exist. What's in your purse? A stick of butter and a tube of lipstick.

GENTS

This is what many a Brooklyn hipster aims to be but never quite achieves. A big, charming smile is said to be a Southern gent's best accessory. But you can't go out with nothing on but a grin.

Bow ties are a must. You must know how to tie that sucker (Hint: It's nothing like a regular tie) and wacky patterns are totally fine. If you get your hands on silk, you're winning.

Light gingham shirts (you know, the ones that look like tablecloths?) are what's hot, and the detail is in the buttons. Nice buttons mean class.

Traditionally, the gingham is swapped out for a crisp white shirt if a cocktail party is in order. The idea is to be comfortable, but to still look good enough to hold a glass of bourbon with finesse.

Pants are tailored down South, jeans must fit well, and you'll need to cuddle up to khakis. Furthermore (and this one's important), get used to going sockless in leather shoes. The heat won't allow you to wear socks on your feet and Southern gents bare their ankles with pride. Alligator belts, cuff links, and nice watches are pieces that speak to heirloom fashion traditions. Double monk strap shoes are a classic; these came from actual European monks who wore them as a more protective alternative to sandals. Oxfords and derby shoes (laced ones) are cool, too. It's all about the "Nice shoes, wanna fuck?" sort of vibe. And shining them is a must.

ATTITUDES

The surface dynamic between belles and gents is a cordial, traditional interaction, and that is reflected in the feminine, overfussy styles. But the South is not impervious to the changing times; some just cling to tradition more than others. Belles are to be sweet and gents are to be chivalrous. Whether this actually happens, that's up for debate. Plus, there are gender-amorphous people all over the world, and in the South, too.

FOOD FOR THE SOUL

Soul food gets its richness from ingredients, a slow cooking process, and a deep history. Soul food digs at the heart of the American South and is a story of making lemonade out of lemons or, rather, meals to feed families from discarded bits and pieces.

WINDOW TO THE SOUL

The 1964 entry for *soul food* in Webster's Dictionary states that its first appearance was in that year, which negates a long history of African-American cooking. While its official name became popular during the civil rights movement, the origins of flavorful greens, beans, cornbread, and one-pot meals are deeply rooted in slavery, a fact that's hard to swallow but cannot be ignored.

Soul food is about sharing, and it's about family. It is empowering to be in control of your own food; it's about autonomy. Slaves were given animal innards, animal feet, and leftover scraps. In combination with the crops they grew, like corn, greens, and beans, they created an entire cuisine that was later incorporated, and at times misappropriated, into mainstream 'Merica.

Slaves were divided into two groups: those who worked the fields and those who

worked inside. Cooking inside the "Big House," with a plethora of ingredients, was very different than what went on inside the slaves' log cabins, where meat was used as flavoring and fried chicken rarely made it to the table. Instead, stews and one-pot meals were concocted to create caloric, filling dishes, served in large portions with the intent to keep a lot of people full for a long time. The use of spices, pickling techniques, and the practice of reducing liquids into gravies made off-cuts of meat and bruised vegetables more palatable. Food that lacked quality was transformed with ingenuity and finesse.

Soul food tasted like home, and once people gained their freedom, the taste of home began to travel, picking up ingredients and popularity along the way. For instance, Gullah (the black people of the low country in South Carolina) used a lot of seafood, and dirty rice became their thing.

Restaurants featuring soulful dishes began sprouting up, eventually reaching as far north as Harlem, New York, where Sylvia's Restaurant, the proprietor of which is known as the "Queen of Soul Food," is still keeping the taste of home alive today.

Oprah once said about slaves that "Their food was a way of surviving with dignity in a very oppressive situation." So what was on the menu?

FRIED CHICKEN

While it was special-occasion fare, reserved only for when whole animals were caught, the soul food version—crisp, sometimes spicy, moist, juicy, and flavorful—was perfected in the South. Rabbits, opossums, fish, and squirrels were more popular on the dinner table then.

ODDS AND ENDS

The soul food kitchen was well stocked with discarded meaty bits like chitlins (intestines) cracklins (skin), pigs' feet, neck bones, hog jowl ("maws"), pigs' ears, and fatback-salted pork. These undesirable parts underwent a remarkable transformation every night in the hands of soulful cooks who applied West African cooking techniques and used meat as flavoring to turn out deeply flavored dishes.

FIXIN'S

Collards, mustard greens, sweet potatoes, black-eyed peas, and corn grown in little plot gardens were typical components of soul food. Some crops were brought over from Africa, and while slaves didn't have anything material, they did bring with them the knowledge of how to cook and work the land for food. Corn, native to America, played an important role in the making of cornbread, grits, and cornmeal for coating, making meals more starchy and substantial. Condiments, like chow-chow (a spicy pickle relish), hot sauce, drippings (cooking juices turned to gravy), and molasses made from reduced sorghum, rounded out the flavors of soul food. Nothing was wasted; nothing was bland.

When you're cooking from snout to tail, but have none of the in-between, you must get creative. People made do and what they did is nothing short of brilliant.

LOW COUNTRY BOIL

The murky waters and the mucky night air of the low country set the perfect scene for a tradition that brings people together around a table covered in boiled bits scattered on butcher paper. It used to be called Frogmore Stew after the birthplace of Richard Gay, a guy who figured out how to feed one hundred soldiers with a one-pot meal. It's not a stew, but more of a melding of seafood and corn, sometimes onions and butter, and is meant to be eaten with your hands. An easy way to feed a lot of people, the low country boil is a social gathering that celebrates the southern coast of 'Merica.

BRING TO A BOIL

The idea is to find the largest container, maybe a garbage can, and some sort of straining mechanism. The water is seasoned with spices and lemon, then ingredients are dropped into the boiling water in order of cooking time, with the shellfish going in toward the end. Everything is then strained and dumped onto a butcher paper–covered table and people go to town ripping off

heads and tails and chowing down. If your fingernails don't get all grimy, you're not doing it right.

While the idea is the same, regional variations throw their own flavors into the boiling pot.

Georgia

Here, a mixture of crab and shrimp, spiced liberally, with halved lemons, sausage, whole potatoes, and chunks of corn is thrown into a Georgia boil. Once the pot is going, it'll be about six hours until the feasting begins. The best thing to do while you wait for everything to meld together in the cauldron of low country flavor is kick back with a few beers and let the summer heat lull you into a chillin' daze. When the table gets its fishy centerpiece dumped onto it, you are expected to liberally dip everything in the butter provided to make Paula Deen proud.

Louisiana

Louisianans are masters of crawfish/crawdads, which are dug out of the bogs in large quantities during the summer. Since sausage goes into everything in New Orleans, you'll find some meaty pieces in the water as well. Getting your boil on here means going head to head with crawdads and sucking out the flavorful parts until it's all shell.

South Carolina

The Carolinas, like their coastal cousins, boil up all kinds of seafood in the summer, but the winter favorite is roasting oysters over a scorching fire. The idea of feeding a lot of people is the same in this winter variation of a boil. Sometimes the plump oysters are roasted over wood chips that impart a smoky flavor. They naturally steam inside because of the shell. People will bear the cold and cuddle up to the roasting oysters for warmth because they just love to cook outside that much.

Northeast variations exist, throwing in whatever seafood swims their way, but the most authentic experience is down South. Something about the drawl makes the low country boil taste a little more like home cookin'.

EAT ALL THE BBQ

To Southerners, their own region's BBQ is the best. You try to dispute that and you'll be holding onto your own burnt ends for dear life. Shit's serious. You can complain about the weather, or the quality of anything else, but don't ever criticize the 'cue. Yanks are really hesitant to talk about different BBQ styles because they imagine some frothy-mouthed Southerner around the corner ready to pounce on how they don't know shit about meat and sauce. Here are the simplest divisions to help you understand the regional differences.

ROOTS

BBQ is actually a form of preserving meat adapted from the Caribbean. It was brought over by Spanish colonists, along with pigs, whose meat is smoked in order to keep it from rotting. Barbecue comes from maximizing the flavor of cheaper cuts of meat, which often contain a lot of connective tissue and fat, by introducing smoke, long cooking times, and flavorful sauces. The South is a culture of taking things slow; you can hear it in the language and you can taste it in the food. Southern BBQ is all about the pig, but moving across regions brings other proteins, as well as regional ingredients, to the party. Tuck a bib into your shirt and let's get down, not stopping until every bone is clean.

THE CAROLINAS

The sauces and ingredients start minimal on the coast and get more complicated the further west you move. In the Carolinas,

it's always about slow-roasting the pig. Pulled pork is how the 'Linas get down. In North Carolina, pork is accented by a thinner, vinegar-based BBQ sauce, while in South Carolina, you'll get a thicker, gold mustard–based sauce. Here, the people wouldn't dare think of sticking a tomato in sauce. Nearby Alabama takes its 'cue from surrounding states, but adds a white sauce and chicken to the mix.

ON THE SIDE: Coleslaw varies from east to west. Creamy slaw complements vinegar-based BBQ sauces in the East, and more vinegary preparations complement BBQ in the West. Hoecakes, or pancake medallions cooked on the flat, hot top of a hoe, make their way onto Carolina plates as well.

OTP Tip: Down South you will see appalling, bright-red pickles on sticks. These are cukes soaked in Kool-Aid and they will haunt your dreams forever.

MEMPHIS

Memphis is also all about pork; dry or wet, this style of BBQ usually consists of ribs on or off the bone, smoked and roasted in a pit for an agonizingly long time (sometimes for days!). The slow cooking is the important part, as it gives the meat a distinctive smoky flavor and texture. Memphians keep their sauce simple and thin (tomatoes, vinegar, spices) so as not to overpower the flavorful meat. Dry rubs are the big deal here, not the sauces.

ON THE SIDE: Spaghetti doused in BBQ sauce, because you can't get as fat as Elvis on meat alone.

KANSAS CITY

This is a style that can be traced back to one guy, Henry Perry, and to a place called Kansas City in Missouri. This style is also about smoke, but with a different approach. Meat is slow-cooked in a pit, then covered in thick syrupy sauce (molasses and tomato) and cooked some more until everything caramelizes. The sweet and spicy burnt ends that result are like meat candy made up of the fatty ends of brisket.

ON THE SIDE: Mac 'n' cheese, French fries, corn, and beans (reinforced with extra-sweet sauce to make them extra-tasty).

TEXAS

Many argue that Texas BBQ isn't the real thing, because Texans focus on grilling beef—but are you really going to argue with a Texan? This take on BBQ follows the old adage that everything is bigger in Texas. So big that Texas actually has four subdivisions of BBQ, splitting the state geographically into East, West, North, and South.

The styles are largely differentiated by the type of wood they use for smoking, and the kind of heat that's applied. The Southern region's proximity to Mexico also throws a bit of Mexican-style barbacoa into the mix. A slab of Texas BBQ steak will feed a family of four, and calling it BBQ may get you a kick in the pants in other parts of the South.

ON THE SIDE: Cornbread, creamy slaw, potato salad, and pinto beans.

BBQ is a (necessarily?) complicated subject. Everyone wants to simplify the different regional styles and grouping them together might get us a good Southern spanking. All you really need to know is that there will be meat, there will be sauce, and it will all put you in a coma.

HOW TO FEST FROM SPRING TO SUMMER

You've heard of SXSW, but Austin isn't the only place in the South that parties hard. Every state delivers its own reasons to dust off the hip flask, put on your booty shorts, and bear the humid heat in the name of hearing some outdoor tunes. Here are five of the best fests to help transition you from spring to summer in the South.

MARCH

Wake up from winter with neon! The Buku Music + Art Project in NOLA features the best touring artists, and the kind of swirly-whirly laser-beam aesthetic you need to remind yourself that brighter days are on the horizon. Will everybody be wacked out on psychedelics? You betcha.

For EDM madness, the Ultra Music Festival takes place in Miami every March and will set you up for the rest of summer. It's the kind of festival that will scramble your brain and bust your eardrums if you're not careful (which you shouldn't be).

APRIL

A fairly new fest that's gaining popularity, the Norman Music Festival in Oklahoma started in 2008 as a one-day ordeal, and has since grown to a two-night festival that attracts bigger and bigger names every year. Some of the artists have included the Dirty Projectors, Portugal the Man, and Ra Ra Riot. Kicking off your summer festing in the warm Oklahoma spring is a good way to get more partying under your belt.

MAY

The Hangout Music Festival in Alabama consists of six stages set up right by the rolling waves of the ocean. Things are bound to hang out at this shoreside fest, which welcomes the likes of TV on the

Radio, the Foo Fighters, Cold War Kids, and My Morning Jacket. There will be crowd surfing, beach balls, bikinis, and saltwater makeout sessions. Sponsors like Coca-Cola and Malibu Rum set up stations to help you stay hydrated and promptly dehydrated, and misting stations are around to cool you off. The hangout lasts three whole days, so bring enough sunscreen to make it to the end without looking like a lobster.

JUNE

Set inside the Mulberry Mountains, the Wakarusa Music and Camping Festival goes down the first week of June in Arkansas and is about as diverse as it gets. Acts like beat heavy Bassnectar are followed by icons like the Flaming Lips, with hip-hop favorites like the Roots on the lineup as well. This grab bag of music comes with some picturesque perks.

The city of Ozark is well known for its natural beauty, and when the speakers shut down for the night, camping, swimming in the river, and hiking in the area are great ways to give your ears a rest.

By the time Bonnaroo rolls around, blasting loud during the second week of June in Tennessee, you should be hitting your festival stride. This one's for the seasoned festgoer. With a Burning Man aesthetic, you spend four days in the barren area of Manchester, populated by candy-colored music-lovers, the air filled with some of the best musicians known to (dirty dirty) man.

BONUS

VANS WARPED TOUR

Every year, this mosh-pit party travels to cities across America, setting up screaming stages. If you're looking for that one person who can't let punk die, you'll find at least five hundred here. The artists are mostly "indie" and the festgoers skew younger (be careful who you put your face on).

THE JUKEBOX

The jukebox changed the way music was heard in the segregated, post-Prohibition era. Speakeasies couldn't afford live bands and putting in a jukebox meant they could still blast music, with the patrons paying for what they wanted to hear. A box that makes you dance, as in a juke house, was a brilliant idea and instrumental in blurring the lines between black and white.

JUKE JOINTS

Juke joints (aka barrel houses) were scattered along the "Chitlin Circuit." The word *juke* comes from the Gullah word *joog*, meaning "wicked." These were places where you'd go to dance, and to be rowdy and disorderly. They were places where newly emancipated slaves partied after the workweek and drank moonshine. Segregation meant black people needed to open their own party spots, usually on roadsides, where hot bodies were packed into tight joints, dancing, sweating, and being merry.

The other side of juke joints was all business. Companies and plantations built on-site party places (in barrel houses) to attract workers. This was also beneficial to the bosses, who could monitor their employees' actions and ensure that a portion of the workers' income would be fed right back into the company. Quite a backhanded perk.

JUKEBOX

While the Great Migration moved six million bodies out of the South, the jukebox dispersed black voices across the country. The Automatic Musical Instrument Company (AMI) created the first recognizable, coin-operated jukebox, and by the 1940s, 75 percent of all records made in America lived inside jukeboxes. Not only did jukeboxes relieve bar owners from having to hire live entertainment, but since the machines kept tabs on which music was played most, they became a big driver for determining popular music (like a primitive form of likes and views on YouTube).

COUNTRY BLUES IN THE CITY

The jukebox brought the faceless sounds of the South to every part of the country. The Mississippi Delta Blues, with its twangy steel guitars and heart-wrenching songs of poverty, was first recorded in the 1920s. While white bar owners would be reluctant to hire a black blues band for the night, popping in a record exposed white people to the voices of black musicians. Black recording artists had the opportunity to gain popularity when their records appeared inside jukeboxes. And while jukeboxes didn't stop segregation and racism in its tracks, they did form musical connections across racial divides.

Today, jukeboxes are a novelty, connected to the Internet. They're there just in case you feel like hearing "Smells Like Teen Spirit" while shooting a round of pool.

THE MUSIC SHRINES OF TENNESSEE

The birthplace of country music, Tennessee is also the place where famous Southern musicians live in immortality. Aside from the collections at the Country Music Hall of Fame and Museum in Nashville, Tennessee is rich with shrines dedicated to beloved music-makers. Here are five that bring the house down every time.

THE JOHNNY CASH MUSEUM

If you've been wearing all black and chain-smoking in hopes of getting your voice down an octave, this place is for you. A collection of bits and pieces of the Man in Black's life tell the story of his epic influence on music, film, and American culture.

Inside, you'll find love letters to June that'll tug on your heartstrings, along with an array of his abstract, moving artwork, and a listening station that plays those sad tunes he's best known for. The Johnny Cash Museum will make you hurt.

WILLIE NELSON AND FRIENDS MUSEUM AND GENERAL STORE

An eclectic collection of country music memorabilia, this place is full of Nashville charm and the General Store has every kind of Willie souvenir you'd ever want. It's a store with a rich party history that used to (illegally) serve Bloody Marys in the middle of the week and put on armadillo races. Famous country faces came through these parts to celebrate album releases and momentous occasions. Not just a shrine to Willie, the museum also features interesting things from other country stars and music history—plus an issue of *Playboy* that's written entirely in Braille.

LORETTA LYNN RANCH

The daughter of a coal miner, Loretta married at fourteen(!), pumped out six kids, picked up a guitar and started belting out country jams for the next fifty years. Her crazy, rocky love life inspired much of her music, which breached feminist topics (like birth control) that kicked up country dust. To contain all this country madness, Loretta settled on a sprawling ranch that for over thirty years played host to racing events, including Lynn's own Amateur Motocross

Racing Championships, the largest in the country. Today, you can visit Loretta's spacious ranch and check out the Coal Miner's Daughter Museum to learn about her life. For spooks, hit the haunted plantation to meet the ghost of a woman who died of grief after losing her newborn.

DOLLYWOOD

Dollywood is an entire theme park resort spotlighting America's favorite busty Southern belle, Dolly Parton. About three million people visit Dollywood every year to take the thrill rides, listen to Smoky Mountain jams, slide around the water park, and ponder how one little lady made such an impact. Before Dollywood, the area was a small theme park, with a few roller

coasters and attractions. While Dolly didn't exactly start this thing, she bought into it in the '80s, and, by putting her name on it, attracted the people traffic needed to make it the success it is today.

GRACELAND

The King will always live on in Graceland, his perfectly preserved home, place of death, and a national historic landmark. Once inside the house, things get really personal. You walk through the rooms, dotted with personal family photos, his baby grand staring at you from the corner, and an eerie kitchen where you know Elvis pigged out on some massive amounts of grub. Get all shook up in the floor-to-ceiling, green-carpeted jungle room—his gaudy, green studio oasis—and wander into his basement, where he likely stubbed his toes on the pool table trying to get to the wet bar. The whole thing is super-kitschy but (somewhat) real; Elvis was a weirdo (remember that sparkly jumpsuit thing?) and his mansion isn't any different. To pay your final respects to Elvis, his grave (along with the graves of his other family members, including his stillborn twin brother) is out in the meditation garden.

If, after hitting these shrines, you still have room for more country good times in Tennessee, you can visit the International Rockabilly Hall of Fame, the Memphis Rock n' Soul Museum, the Music Valley Wax Museum, the honky-tonks of lower Broadway, and, of course, the Grand Ole Opry.

=== *Fun Fact* ===

Elvis's foul-mouthed aunt Delta continued to live at the estate and use the kitchen in the private wing (which is now open to the public) until 1993.

AUSTIN: IN TEXAS
BUT NOTHING LIKE TEXAS AT ALL

While you may find a stray ten-gallon hat around these parts, it'll likely be decked out in glitter, with a hole cut out for the unicorn horn, atop the head of someone with a ukulele in one hand and an artisan Tex-Mex nacho plate from a food truck in the other; they may or may not be wearing pants.

Austin is so wonderfully different from the rest of Texas. How? Settle on down while we explore the walking contradiction that is Austin, y'all.

THE MANY FESTS OF AUSTIN

While all the other Texans are buckin' their broncos and singing about BBQ stains on their shirts, Austin is blowing it up with a festival schedule that'll keep you entertained by big names and weird folks alike.

Aside from SXSW—the mega collaboration of music, film, tech, and art that takes over the city for two weeks in March—Austin throws down festivals all summer long and beyond. The Euphoria Fest in April is a rave with a bunch of drugs and half-naked hippies camping under the stars. Want reggae instead of EDM? There's a fest for that, too: The Austin Reggae Festival takes place the following weekend. More beer, less ganja? The Untapped Festival Austin takes place the

weekend after that (with likely the same amount of ganja, but a bunch of craft beer in the mix, too).

Come May, there's the Levitation Festival (formerly the Austin Psych Fest), which brings to town huge acts, like the Flaming Lips, and local bands (with ridiculous names). And in August, suit up for Bat Fest, an event featuring fest favorites, like music and food, all dedicated to the emergence of a million bats from under a bridge. Start wrapping it up with the Austin City Limits Fest with the likes of the Foo Fighters, Drake, and Deadmau5 for two weekends in October.

Before going home for the holidays, squeeze just one more fest into November. The Fun Fun Fun Fest delivers on its triplicate name with indie and big touring artists alike, plus great food, "action sports," and poster art experiences.

Since it's almost always hot as fuck, partying is a way of telling the heat you ain't sweatin' it. Moral of the story: Buy a tent, stay a while.

WAIT, VEGAN AND BBQ?

In other parts of Texas, vegans are a sickly bunch, damned to go to hell for shunning beef and bacon. But Austin gladly takes the lonely vegetable-eaters under its wing. Consistently named the best city in 'Merica to be vegan (by PETA no less), Austin sports an array of vegan restaurants from tacos to fine dining, and from food carts to trucks (Freeto Pie at Yacht!). They also have home-brewed products like Malk (nut milk), vegan grocery stores, and Vida Vegan Con, an entire convention reserved for cruelty-free Texans (and meatless visitors).

When the vegans are all tucked in at night, Austin throws a big ol' meat party. In addition to great BBQ all over the city (it is Texas, after all), Live Fire is a celebration of beef that's simply about chefs, fire, and meat. Every year, chefs from popular BBQ joints gather to grill their offerings, some of which are gussied up foodie dishes, while others are whole and true to the hearty traditions of Texas.

AND TEX-MEX?

Tex-Mex is perhaps the sole reason why Americans think that eating things like crunchy taco shells with ground cat food, chopped iceberg lettuce, and Velveeta cheese is a trip deep into the exotic land of Mexico. Truth of the matter is, Tex-Mex is not authentic Mexican. Well, not all of it. It's hard to pull apart which parts are Texan, which are Mexican, and which are an animal all on their own. From tacos to queso dip, and carnitas to chili con carne, Austin's got this fusion thing down cold, plus a whole lot of ridiculous nachos, piled high with as many nonvegetables as you possibly can (and maybe can't) stomach.

ALL KINDS OF SEX

If the shape of the Austin Motel (Hint: It's a giant, glowing penis) doesn't tip you off, Austin likes to get down. Aside from the fact that the heat will strip everybody down to body paint most days, there are events like the Air Sex Show (air guitar, minus guitar, plus thrusting), clothing-optional Hippie Hollow Park, an array of nonskeezy sex shops and strip clubs, and the most accepting attitude toward whatever sex, gender, or fetish you're into this side of the Mason-Dixon line.

OTP Tip: If you're going to get filthy on Dirty 6th (the part of town with all the wild bars), wearing "protection" means wearing both condoms and shoes.

SHIT'S JUST WEIRD HERE

How weird, you ask?

1. There's an old hippie named Carl. He's known for his man boobs.

2. They have celebrated Eeyore's (yeah, the donkey) birthday since 1977 with an outdoor party that involves hula hoops, drum circles, weed, booze, and honey sandwiches. Most people are costumed; some are topless.

3. Rot (Republic of Texas) Rally: bikers, neon-bikini "babes," noise, and madness.

4. People take pride in the art they create in their yards, which can range from hubcap sculptures to stuffed animal scenes to stone dinosaurs.

5. They shun anything corporate and "keep Austin weird" by being hyperlocavores: eating, drinking, dressing, buying and listening to music, locally. The good kind of weird.

TAILGATING LIKE A PRO

Tailgating is pregaming taken to such an extreme that it needs its own name—and a truck. Would you believe it goes back to ancient harvest festivals? Neither can we. But we do know that this is how 'Merica prefers to prepare for a football game.

THE AMERICAN TAILGATERS ASSOCIATION

Yes, there is such a thing!

It may have started when wagons filled with food, wine, and whiskey rolled into the First Battle of Bull Run/Manassas in 1861 in Virginia during the Civil War. Another theory is that the first true tailgaters were those partying at the Rutgers versus Princeton game of 1869. The cold hard facts aren't necessary. A really cold beer, however, is crucial.

College games didn't sell booze, and to exercise our American right to goddamnit drink beer and get hyped, tailgating was born. Yale is popular for both tailgating and also cracking down on tailgating. At the pro level, everyone can agree that tailgating started with the Packers in Green Bay, but the Southeastern Conference (we're looking at you, Gators) does the tailgate best.

HOW TO WIN AT TAILGATING

Game-Day Food

First and foremost, you will have to start eating and drinking at 9 a.m. The food at a tailgate is serious business, and every region has their favorites. The rules are that the food must feed a stampede of football fans, it must be greasy, preferably grilled, and it should be the perfect complement to the pissy undertones of shit beer. Charcoal grills and burgers will always get play, no matter where you are. And people like to BBQ, then brag about how their BBQ is the best BBQ.

Prekickoff Coolers

Learn to open that back part of your throat because, before kickoff, you'll be reaching in that beer cooler quite a lot. Don't sit on the cooler; bring a tailgating chair; and don't sit on other people's tailgating chairs. People normally trade burgers for beers and beers

for sodas, but never beers for whiskey. Each person should contribute to the lot, and not just a 40 of O.E., either. This is community building! Your cooler must have the perfect water-to-ice-to-beer ratio. If you take out a beer, you offer a beer.

Hooking Up

Tailgates happen at college games, and you know who cares about college games? College students (and the occasional forty-year-old Old Schooler, or your dad looking to share father-son bonding tailgating moments). You go to tailgates to make new drinking bro friends and bond in many ways; just don't get your tongue tied across opposing team enemy lines. Trash talking is sometimes like kindergarten flirting but sometimes it escalates into violence, so check your testosterone at the parking lot entrance.

Tricked-Out Trucks

You'll need a tailgate—that little back part of a truck that flips down. In this case, to unveil all your party glory (beer, food, etc.) and create a little bench. Favorable vehicle features include a loud stereo, flip-down seats, video screens, a flatbed, a tow hook for your grill, a built-in fridge, and the kind of truck that packs up easily once it's time for the game. This is a parking lot, after all. Be able to fit folding everythings—chairs,

tables, origami—into the truck. If you can fold it, you should bring it.

The Team Experience

If Americans are anything, they're ridiculously hard-core football fans. The goal is to become a vulgar extension of your favorite team in the parking lot. Adopt the feeling of being part of the competition without having any athletic skills or status. Do you really need to know anything about football? No. Just scream when people around you scream and you should be fine, or dead—one of the two. Creating your own entertainment in addition to the entertainment provided for you is encouraged, because it will make the whole experience feel more participatory. As such, games will be part of the fun: Cornhole, flip cup, beer pong, horseshoes—basically anything where something can be thrown at something else (on parking lot concrete) is fair game, Solo cup or not.

Tailgating has gotten commercialized: Companies (or the NFL) come in and set up organized parties, where you meet cheerleaders and watch the game on the big screen. But that's not the essence of tailgating; that's capitalism. You're supposed to get drunk, paint your face, bro out to the max, and be secretly happy to have partied, even if your team loses. It's DIY organized chaos with maritime laws.

HEDONISM IN MIAMI

While the rest of Florida is securely the South, Miami is an exception, with a culture that revolves around tans and tits with Cuban flair. Hedonism is all about pleasure and indulgence, and Miami is the place for such pursuits. You'll need something neon, with or without glitter, a grasp of Spanglish, and an appetite for champagne (in your mouth and on your person) to get down in the 305. Here's how Miami gets its heady dose of hedonism.

DOWN THOSE DRANKS

Downing an indulgent amount of champagne is a requisite in Miami. When not dipping into the bubbly, this town gets down on sugary drinks with enough umbrellas and fruit decorations to unravel your bikini. From bright white piña coladas—loaded with coconut rum and the consistency of sunscreen—to sticky mint mojitos, Miami is the place to let your love for girly drinks fly high. The appropriately named Miami Vice—a half daiquiri, half piña colada—is your fast train to Drunk Town. To really push the ticket on hedonistic drinking, the Coronita is a concoction that's only okay in Miami. A giant margarita with two Coronas shoved into it for good measure, this drink will give you sea legs and immediately wipe your memory clean.

DIRTY DANCING

Miami's hot club today is its shithole the next, but its party scene, while always changing, is a sweaty storm of all-night dirty dancing. Several clubs have survived the test of time. LIV (roman numeral for 54) is about as posh and show-offy as it gets; getting a table here is a big deal.

The Mansion is all about fancy dancing to keep up with nipple-tassled go-go girls. The horniest of mega clubs has to be the Mokai Lounge, where vintage porno flicks tease you from the screens.

Perhaps the most hedonistic dance party is the patio at Club Space. You will come here on Sunday to a freak show and not leave until your limbs feel like they're made of iron. You'll sleep when you're dead and, if you die in Miami, an occasional hip thrust will be heard from inside your coffin.

OTP Tip: In between indulgences, visit a bit of party history out in the stilts. Stiltsville is a grouping of little shacks in the middle of the water that used to be the place moonshiners partied while smuggling rum onto the mainland.

GET LAID WITH EASE

Miami is made for sex-dulgences and it's pretty easy to go from casual to naked (assuming you're not already casually naked to begin with). Down in South Beach (SoBe), you'll find copious pool parties and bumpin' hotel bars that are practically built for hooking up. The Venetian Pool is the largest freshwater pool in America and the amount of Miami nakedness that goes on here is unreal. Once you've bonded with a gyrating body by the pool, hotel rooms are a stone's throw away, which makes getting horizontal a Miami breeze.

BEACH BINGE

It's hot and humid year-round, so the best thing to do is take off all your clothes and get into a body of water with like-minded hedonists. The obvious destination is South Beach, where the beach binging has been going strong for decades. Festivals here almost always pour out onto the beach, with the Winter Gay Festival taking over the sand into the wee hours of the hot, hot night. Venture down the South Beach stretch until you hit Haulover Park, where you'll find acres of white sand, 1.5 miles of shoreline, and the largest nude beach in the country.

GLUTTONOUS GRUB

When the liquid and powder diet becomes stomach-curdlingly painful, Miami will feed you all the right stuff to get you back on your feet (or back on your back). Indulge in stone crabs at Joe's, sensual ceviche at SuViche, and heavy-but-hot cubano sandwiches at El Palacio de los Jugos. Chase it all down with coconut juice extracted via machete and you should be good to go another hedonistic round in this fair city.

IVE REAL HEADLINES THAT PROVE FLORIDA iS F*CKING NUTS

What the hell is going on in Florida? Why are people eating each other's faces off and calling the cops to ask for Kool-Aid and weed? Something must be in that gator-infested water that's making Florida all wonky. People down here will bite you for even minor infractions and stab you for less. Here's a small taste of the wacky shit that makes the news in Florida.

Man Stabbed in Confusion over Harmonicas

Herald Tribune, Sarasota, February 27, 2012

So, Old Dude picks up Guy at a bar Saturday, they head over to Taco Bell and buy a bag of tacos. When the passenger grabs the bag to get out of the car, Old Dude stabs him in the wrist and chest while yelling, "Give me my harmonicas!" Because in Florida, touching a man's (bag of??) harmonicas is grounds for a blood battle.

Babysitter Accused of Sleeping on Toilet as Two-Year-Old Wanders to Canal with Alligators

TCPalm, Palm Beach, April 10, 2009

Florida has gators. If the toddler wandered anywhere, there would be gators there. Just a fact of life. Pretty self-explanatory except for the part about falling asleep on the john. We've done our fair share of sleeping in odd places, but with a two-year-old in your care, it's probably a good idea to be more alert when your pants are down.

Thieves Kill Family's Pet Turkey for Thanksgiving Meal

Channel 10 News, Tampa Bay, November 21, 2012

Christa and Brian had fifty animals on their property in Gulf Breeze, of which their favorite was Tom, the thirty-pound turkey that Christa said was just like "having a normal family dog." What do you do when the supermarket is all out of birds for the big day? Find some friendly neighbors and hack their turkey to pieces, which is exactly what two dudes with a pickup did, with a bow and arrow nonetheless. These guys were grateful for many things that Thanksgiving, none more than having animal-hoarder neighbors.

Florida Woman Causes Two Vehicle Crashes While Shaving Her Bikini Line

Keys News, Key West, May 8, 2010

Megan and her ex-husband are in a car. She's driving/shaving her bikini line, he's steering from the backseat. She was getting ready to see her new boyfriend and we all know a fuzzy bikini line is a big no-no. Why not do it in the shower? Multi-tasking people! If you're going to do it in the car, maybe let the ex-husband drive? It all would have made perfect sense if just a few things were tweaked, or waxed. Wait, why is the ex-husband there again? Oh yeah, steering.

Fake Doctor Injected Fix-a-Flat and Cement into Patient's Butt

Miami News, Miami Beach, November 18, 2011

This headline made its way around the Internet and went viral because it was just so fucking absurd. Cement is cheaper than silicone, so why not just do a clean swap and inject industrial building materials into people's butts? Technically, you are fixing a flat.

BONUS

Dumb Blonde Joke Ends in Nipple Bite, Knife Attack

NBC 6 South Florida, Miami, July 4, 2011

If you're going to make jokes about people being dumb, make sure they're smart enough not to bite you.

THE YANKEES

When people think of the East Coast, cities like New York City, Philadelphia, and Washington, D.C. probably come to mind. In addition to homey New England, old-ass architecture, and a certain city grime, Yankee territory is also covered in wild terrain, like gorgeous snowy spots in Vermont, the Adirondacks, and some surprisingly kick-ass beaches with monstrous waves. America's presidents have called D.C. home; railroad riches financed the giant mansions of Newport, Rhode Island; and many a drunkard passes out daily on the streets of New York. Cozy up to our favorite bro bars in Boston, fill up on wings in Buffalo, and stop by Maine for the lobster of a lifetime.

THE FIVE BEST SURF SPOTS ON THE EASTERN SEABOARD

Surfing in 'Merica isn't just reserved for those goddamn hippies out West. While the waves in the East are fewer and less consistent and the water is colder, surfing the Atlantic on the Eastern Seaboard is thrilling. Hitting the coastline during hurricane season is best, as those choppy waves stir up the most action. Suit up and get ready to be thrown around by some aggressive East Coast waters.

MANASQUAN INLET, NEW JERSEY

The waves here break fast and attract clique-y surfers who are used to getting thrown around together. Hurricane Sandy in 2012 wiped out visitors to this place for a while, but those who trickled back in demand respect. Nearby Point Pleasant is great for kayaking, and the Sedge Islands, which can be accessed through the wildlife tour, are Jersey's first marine life reserve.

SEA ISLE CITY, NEW JERSEY

This spot is great for beginners, as the waves are small and steady. When you've mastered the waters here, lie on the pillowy

sand or hit the Heritage Surf & Sport, which has been around since '64, teaching all the little Jerseyans the art of surfing.

OTP Tip: If you want more Jersey Shore, try out Allenhurst and Ocean City.

MONTAUK, NEW YORK

Driving out to Montauk from Manhattan parallels the feeling of stripping off layers until you get to the gooey center. With every mile, the madness disappears and the roads become more singular and desolate, especially in the winter. When you get to the tip of Montauk, you'll be presented with a coastline filled with reefs, coves, and points. The waves are consistent but the town's population swells and ebbs drastically, depending on the season.

Fun Fact

The Montauk Monster is a raccoon-like thing that washed ashore in 2008. Many have theorized what in fuck this thing is, and some say it came from Plum Island, where there's an animal testing facility.

NEWPORT, RHODE ISLAND

Ruggles is well known by the hard-core surfer community as an intense surf spot, with huge waves breaking over jagged rocks. This spot is best for those who have slid into a barrel before; if you're just trying to stay on the board, Ruggles will slap you straight onto your ass. Ruggles is known to hold twenty-foot wave faces, and the best way to get here is to take the steps down to the beach from the Cliff Walk, a 3.5-mile historic coastline stroll that takes you through scenic parts of Newport.

RYE ON THE ROCKS, NEW HAMPSHIRE

While you *can* sip a rye on these rocks, it's best to take them on sober. Rye on the Rocks is a showcase of the best New England has to offer. The left-to-right waves are rough and sometimes slam right into the exposed rock reef. It'll look like a giant washing machine if you don't know your shit, and it'll feel like a roller coaster if you do. If getting sucked into barrels is your thing, this is the place for you. While the locals are New England–nice, when the waves get rolling, it's every human for him- or herself.

TAKE ON THE ADIRONDACKS

Just a skip up from Manhattan, a slew of adventures abound in the six-million-acre wilderness of Adirondack Park. Leave your party shoes behind and strap on your hiking boots. Trade the skyscrapers for breathtaking cliffs and overpriced drinks for roaring rapids. The thrills around these navigable bodies of water and glorious landscapes will make your Manhattan bar-hopping adventures seem like child's play.

WHITEWATER RAFTING

The Hudson River Gorge is a monster where great waters collide. With water temps hitting seventy degrees in the summer and a water level that goes up to 5.3 feet, sticking your oar into these rapids will be warm and exhilarating. The river features Class III rapids with manageable rippling waves, and Class IV Givneys' Rift will rip your teeth out if you're not careful. If you can handle colder water, come here at the beginning of the season, when the ice has just melted and the water is furious. Kayaking, tubing, canoeing, and stand-up paddling are also great ways to get wet here.

BOULDERING

Bouldering is when you strip off all equipment and just go at it with your bare hands. While the Adirondacks offer many a boulder to grab, the best rocks are around McKenzie Pond. The area has been heavily explored by roaming fingers, but its popularity doesn't compromise its quality. The rocks are sharp and clean, the landings are safe, and the climbs have a good range of difficulty for beginners and calloused experts.

HIKING

The Adirondacks contain forty-six mountains that exceed a 4,000-foot elevation. The "high peaks" hiking possibilities are practically limitless. Many of the trails aren't officially established, but are fairly navigable. For a challenge, the Marcy and Algonquin Mountains are the top dogs. Marcy boasts a fifteen-mile round-trip hike, and at 5,344 feet it is the highest peak in New York state. If you're a fan of fun mountain names, Nippletop is a popular

destination, where the views are spectacular and the beaver pond at the base seals the deal.

OTP Tip: If you fancy yourself a mountaineer, camp around Lake Placid. The area contains forty of the high tops so you can go at it for weeks. Just watch out for the movie-made lake monsters.

EXTREME TREETOP ADVENTURES

The "extreme" part is a bit of an exaggeration, but the treetop obstacle courses here are definitely challenging. There are six adult, color-coded courses, progressing from beginner to ass-kicking, with ten to seventeen obstacles each, and to get through the 1.5-mile adventures, you'll need a lot of upper body strength. When you're done ziplining, tight and slack rope walking, climbing ladders, getting across wobbly bridges, Tarzan swinging, and letting gravity get you through the "Leap of Faith"—a drop off a ledge where you swing into a vertical net—your arms will burn with the fire of taking on the wild and winning.

VERMONT SNOW SPORTS

The Northeast Kingdom is the epitome of New England wilderness, with moose roaming around and mountain lakes aplenty. This isn't the Swiss Alps, but you'll be surprised by how many great snowy peaks and valleys there are in Vermont. With forty-three nordic and alpine resorts to choose from, suitable for all levels and whatever apparatus you like to use to slide down the mountain, here are Vermont's five snowiest slopes.

KILLINGTON

The "Best of the East" offers the highest elevation (4,241 feet) in Vermont, the longest vertical drop (at over 3,000 feet) in the East, and the longest season (late October to mid-May). With six mountains and 155 trails, try your snowy foot at the Juggernaut, a 6.2-mile-stretch of nothing but slope. They're so confident about their snow here (an average of 250 inches, plus some human-made muscle if they need it) that if you're not happy with the coverage, they'll give you a voucher for another visit.

STOWE MOUNTAIN

Kill two mountains in one with 116 trails for the somewhat experienced snow enthusiast. You can gondola between Mount Mansfield and Spruce Peak, while the picturesque 485 skiable acres roll by below. There are thirteen mile-long lifts, some that move fast enough to get your feet planted on the ground again in no time. The surrounding town has an Aspen vibe and some come here to expend energy on the slopes and cash money on the streets.

MOUNT SNOW RESORT

Mount Snow Resort comprises eighty trails that range in difficulty. Carinthia, on the main face, has nine terrain parks (the only one of its kind in the East) with rails, jumps, and a superpipe. Strap on that snowboard and pretend you're a pro or forget the board and hop on a husky sleigh ride. The dogs do the work and you kick back and watch the snowy wonderland like some sort of Russian prince(ss). It's also the closest resort to big cities like Boston (2.5 hours) and NYC (4 hours).

Fun Fact

Since 2007, millions of dollars have gone into the renovation and installation of snow guns here, making for even ground cover no matter what Mother Nature throws your way.

STRATTON MOUNTAIN RESORT

While there are lots of beginner options on Stratton's ninety-seven trails, this mountain is known for its black diamond (and double blacks, if you can handle them) and six terrain parks. The East Byrnes terrain park was designed by sexy Olympic snowboarders Ross Powers and Lindsey Jacobellis, and promises to bring out the snow beast in you. With 670 acres of land, you'll need to try really hard to put a dent in these pristine grounds. Once you're nice and spent, the resort has hot tubs, a huge pool, and steam rooms to get the feeling back in your toes.

SMUGGLER'S NOTCH

Up on Madonna Mountain, the pointed tits of Smuggs is home to "Black Hole," the only triple black diamond in town. The billowing, snow-heavy branches of the pine trees surrounding the slope's 53-degree pitch will put the blackest kind of fear in your heart. Feel free to follow tradition and smuggle illegals in your snowsuit up to/down from Canada so you can have a nice shoulder to cry on. It's touted as a kid-friendly destination, but you'll be too busy ripping through difficult terrain to notice.

OTP Tip: If you like your snow mixed with sun, check out the south-facing trails of Bromley Mountain Resort.

NIAGARA FALLS ON YOU!

A mammoth of a natural attraction, Niagara Falls brings in more than thirty million visitors every year. Massive crowds and surrounding commercial strips can easily crap on your date with nature, but there's still a way to navigate Niagara correctly.

RESPECT THE FLOW

Niagara Falls dumps a collective six million pounds of water every second—the heaviest flow rate on the planet, and damn impressive for a snubbed world wonder. This brute natural strength inspired the world's first hydroelectric power plant in the late 1800s, and still sends power across North America. So apart from providing an epic selfie background, the constant rush of Niagara Falls was probably responsible for powering your phone before breakfast.

=== *Fun Fact* ===

Niagara Falls is a true force of nature, but humankind has managed to once again tame the beast by diverting half the water flow for hydroelectric power. The falls flow at this reduced rate after dusk and during the off-season winter months, but the world's largest faucet gets cranked back up when the crowds come out.

BORDER DEBATE

Niagara Falls is made up of three individual waterfalls that span the Canada-U.S. border: Horseshoe Falls on Canadian turf, with Bridal Veil and American Falls spilling into States territory. The debate over which side is better will live on for as long as water from the Niagara River keeps falling (we're willing to bet on another fifty thousand years or so). Plain and simple, the panoramic views are undeniably superior from the Canadian side. Our Canuck neighbors have created an entire city with rotating restaurants, glowing casinos, and skyrise hotels set to the backdrop of Niagara Falls. If a proper full landscape view is your no. 1 priority, grab a hockey stick and cross the border.

The American side has far less chaos—specifically the parents with strollers kind—and is much better suited for a laid-back picnic, where you can gush over the scene. Engulfed by Niagara Falls State Park (America's oldest), there's a more natural and intimate feel to the 'Merican side, and you can actually get within arm's length of where the river breaks and the water falls. Each side can be accessed via the Rainbow Bridge that connects the two countries, and both run boat tours that'll leave you soaked.

OTP Tip: The Maid of the Mist, the premier tour boat of the falls, leaves every half hour from the United States; its Canadian counterpart is the Hornblower Niagara Cruise.

DON'T GET TRAPPED

The Canadian city of Niagara Falls—arguably the country's greatest tourist trap—will probably leave you in greater awe than the actual waterfalls. Wax museums, street magicians, fudge factories, a Ferris wheel, six haunted house attractions, and even a

Ripley's Believe It or Not! all sprawl down Clifton Hill (or, as the city refers to it, the Street of Fun) in a cash-grab effort that can turn your day trip into a living nightmare. Don't lose sight of what brought you to Niagara Falls (the natural wonder) in the first place. Keep out of this town's many tourist traps or risk joining the dozens of daredevils who decided to barrel down the waterfalls just so they never have to sniff another sweaty hot dog line fart again.

HOW TO SURVIVE A NOR'EASTER

Every year, the weather plays a very cruel joke on Eastern states. It's called a "nor'easter," or a megastorm that blows in and promises apocalyptic-type destruction. The weathermen freak out, everyone says good-bye to their loved ones, and prepares to hide out until the coast is clear. Should you find yourself in this cold predicament, follow the rules below to ensure your survival.

STOCK UP

Buy all the milk and bread! Canned beans and peanut butter would be much better options, since they'll keep forever, but every year the store shelves in the East run out of milk and bread first. People stand in lines for the last loaf as if they're in Mother Russia and refuse to acknowledge any other food groups.

POWER-FREE ACTIVITIES

Possible power outages mean no Netflix; you might have to (gasp) read a book by candlelight. Or come up with some way to pass the time without tech devices. Just remember that if you're stuck indoors in a city like Brooklyn, you share walls with many a neighbor. This means that riding a tricycle indoors while screaming bloody murder is a dick move, because everyone has no choice but to listen to your madness.

DRUNKEN DOWNTIME

Buy all the booze, play drinking games, and have as much sex as possible. It's the right thing to do under such dire circumstances.

EAT ICE CREAM

For some inexplicable reason, whenever the weather drops to hypothermia levels, people in the East go down on tubs of ice cream. Maybe it's a reminder of summer or a rebel move that says, "Fuck you, winter! You're not gonna make me eat soup for four months!" Whatever drives people to reach for that spoon, during a nor'easter the comfort of a pint of Cherry Garcia is unparalleled.

GET A TRASH CAN LID READY

Once you finally emerge from hiding, everything will be covered in the fluffy white stuff. You and everyone you know will be outside fashioning anything flat into a sled. Grab the trash-can lid and celebrate your ability to stick it to the storm.

ALL-AMERICAN MUSEUMS, WASHINGTON, D.C.

Of course you'll have to hit the Lincoln Memorial, the White House, the Washington Monument, and other historical 'Merican sites, but our nation's capital is also a gathering of (often free) museums that explain some of the craziness that is 'Merica. From famous portraits, to spies and the original star-spangled banner, here are the top spots in D.C. to visit for some all-American museum going.

NATIONAL MUSEUM OF AMERICAN HISTORY

It really doesn't get more 'Merican than this place. Everything you've ever wanted to know about this land, from sea to shining sea across the decades, is here for your exploring pleasure. Want to see the original star-spangled banner? The museum has three million national treasures, from Duke Ellington's sheet music to Dorothy's ruby red slippers. You can explore how transportation moved America westward, test your Civil War knowledge, gaze at Lincoln's top hat, and learn all about this kooky country through its quirky remains.

NATIONAL PORTRAIT GALLERY

Next door, you'll find a gathering of famous mugs. Whether in the form of paintings or sculptures, caricatures, or super-serious stills, all the famous American faces live here. From George Washington to Marilyn Monroe, you'll find a face to mock from wall to wall. When you've had your fill of face, chill out in the Kogod Courtyard, a recognized architectural marvel encased in a glass canopy ideal for contemplation.

THE CASTLE

Formally known as the Smithsonian Institution, this redstone, twelfth century–inspired, Romanesque-ish architectural beast is a super-fancy information center. It seems like a waste of space in the age of the Internet, and that's a good thing. The castle gets less foot traffic than surrounding sites,

and its halls, gardens, and chambers are spectacular places to take a breather from the crowds. Among the dead silence, you'll also find an actual dead dude, as the north entrance houses the crypt of James Smithson, the Smithsonian's founding father.

INTERNATIONAL SPY MUSEUM

The one thing that has survived across America's history is a tendency to be paranoid as fuck. If it's not the Russians, it's the Japanese, and if it's not the Japanese, it's those damn Cubans, plotting something on that little music-crazed island. This museum houses every scheme, apparatus, and tall tale ever told in this fair nation. If you fancy yourself a James Bond connoisseur, you won't be disappointed by the artifacts in this collection. The epitome of espionage, the Spy Museum will teach you about the most illustrious international spies, the grandest of sneaky plans, and even explain our fruitless hunt for weapons of mass destruction. At the gift shop, it's "all the spy you can buy," which includes gadgets like pen camcorders, USB cuff links, and watch phones.

PEOPLE'S CRIBS

You know you're extra-famous when your home turns into a museum once you kick the bucket. Such is the case for various figures in U.S. history. During the height of the Civil War, Lincoln lived in a cottage in Washington, D.C., for a quarter of his presidency; that's where he developed the Emancipation Proclamation. You can even pop in to check out Lincoln's crusty old slippers on display at the preserved gothic revival house. Pay Woodrow Wilson a visit in the Kalorama–Embassy Row area and stroke your chin until you come up with peacekeeping strategies in his formal garden. Stop off at the Sewall-Belmont House and Museum, and sit in the "seat of women's suffrage." This house is maintained by the National Woman's Party (NWP) and is dedicated to telling the stories of women's struggles for equality.

SEASIDE AMERICANA

No matter how old you are, that scratched-up vintage carnival aesthetic always conjures up nostalgia. The good ol' days were filled with a certain sense of freedom and fun, when shaky roller-coaster rides cost a dime and the county fair meant cotton candy, games, and carefree merriment. Unique pieces of vintage Americana are scattered around the boardwalks of the Eastern Seaboard, and these are our favorite old-school seaside attractions.

PINBALL, ASBURY PARK, NEW JERSEY

Aside from mingling with the shifty shore people, this hands-on-levers museum, which sits out on the boardwalk and overlooks the Atlantic, is the best way to spend a day. The Silverball Museum is the lifelong collection of Rob Ilvento, Jersey's "pinball wizard." The museum is crammed with more than two hundred machines, most in working order. For a $20 day pass, you can try your hand at the primitive pinball, a box with a rolling ball and pins, and advance through the ages, where colors, lights, music, and elaborate art were added to create the modern machine. The way Silverball is designed tells a story of American gaming history; the museum includes machines from the mod '50s to the psychedelic '60s and up to the *Addams Family*-lovin' '90s, as you make your way around the collection.

CAROUSEL, WESTERLY, RHODE ISLAND

The Watch Hill area of Westerly, Rhode Island, is a summertime spot for families. And while this carousel gets a lot of toddler action because it's designed for riders under twelve, we're not above shoving a few kids aside to snag a ride. The oldest carousel of its kind in America, this slightly creepy ride consists of twenty horses, each equine body carved from a single block of wood and suspended on chains. The carousel was originally part of a traveling carnival, then powered by an actual horse with accompanying music provided by a hand-cranked organ. Left behind in 1879, the attraction has survived hurricanes, was updated to run on water power and then electric power, and was declared a national historic landmark in 1987.

OTP Tip: Don't look too closely at the horses' faces unless you want to have zombie horse nightmares for the rest of your life.

ARCADES, JENKINSON'S, POINT PLEASANT BEACH, NEW JERSEY

Remember the days when your only concern was how many quarters you could collect so you could play the day away at the arcade? That feeling can be yours again at the arcades at Jenkinson's in Point Pleasant Beach, New Jersey. Shoot 'em up basketball, stuffed animals trapped under a giant claw, Skee-Ball, and all the jingling coin sounds you can handle abound at the four retro arcades along the boardwalk. Remember that the goal is to get as many tickets as possible, fold them up all haphazardly, and then trade them in for necessities, like eraser toppers, Tootsie Rolls, and stuffed off-brand cartoon animals.

ZOLTAR, CONEY ISLAND, BROOKLYN, NEW YORK

If we learned one thing from the movie *Big*, it's that you never ask Zoltar for advice you can't handle. We're both terrified and fascinated by this fortune-telling machine, and amid the carney madness of Coney Island, this is one piece of Americana you can't miss. Pop in a dollar and let Zoltar take your life into his purple pimp ring-adorned hands. Who knows? You might end up inhabiting Tom Hanks's body for a while and be magically endowed with the power to tap out tunes with your feet on a giant floor piano.

OTP Tip: No trip to Coney Island would be complete without a stomach-churning Nathan's hot dog. If you can get seventy down the gullet in under ten minutes, consider entering the world-famous hot dog eating contest held annually here on the Fourth of July.

=== *Fun Fact* ===

The original Zoltar was destroyed by Hurricane Sandy in 2012. Think of this version as Zoltar's twin brother, Teddy.

BUMPER CARS, ENFIELD, CONNECTICUT

Some of our fondest childhood memories include ramming people with cars until everyone walked away with whiplash. In Enfield, Connecticut, the fine people at Whirlyball add the (dubiously) popular Spanish sport of jai alai to indoor bumper cars, and let you BYOB. The whole thing looks like some dingy '70s classroom, and playing the lacrosse/basketball hybrid, with bumper cars and open containers of booze on your lap, seems like a recipe for disaster. But if your childhood bumper-car memories need an adult redux, this has to be the best way to spice things up. This one's not quite seaside, but no other place does it (whatever "it" is) quite like this.

TABOO TO TATTOO

Strolling around NYC, you'd be hard-pressed to find a body sans ink. You'd think that the stuff has been under people's skins since the beginning of time. Which it has, but only legally since 1997! This was about the time when Green Day was blowing up, and the year after Tupac died. But just because it wasn't legal didn't mean that people weren't getting pricked left and right. New York's ink battles had some interesting barbershop beginnings, and even underground the ink kept flowing freely in this city of self-expression.

THE BOWERY: BARBERS AND NEEDLES

At the turn of the twentieth century, it was common to come into the shop for a cut-and-tat combo. Barbers were also considered doctors and, in addition to hair-cutting, shaving, and tatting, barbers would also pull teeth, bandage wounds, fix broken bones, put leeches on bar-fight black eyes, and perform the kind of crazy procedures you find in old medical books. Since black eyes were a big disadvantage for day workers, in addition to penning sailboats and buxom beauties, tattoo artists would fix up black eyes with permanent makeup.

> ===== *Fun Fact* =====
>
> The barber's spinning pole colors included blue for veins, red for blood, and white for bandages.

EARLY INK

While early tattoo artists worked free-hand with just a needle and ink, Samuel O'Reilly was the first to patent the tattoo machine in 1891, which was a redesign of Thomas Edison's electric pen. From then, the professional pricking began. The Bowery became a mecca of ink, and artists like Charlie Wagner set up a tattoo parlor behind a barbershop and began perfecting the craft. Artists learned from each other and ventured out on their own.

William Moskowitz was a Russian barber who set up an ink business in the basement below his Bowery barbershop. Willie taught his sons the craft and the family remains a prominent tattoo dynasty until this day. With groups of drunken sailors, barbers, and half-assed surgeons hanging out and getting tatted, tattooing became a macho art form. The grandmother of tattooing, Millie Hull, worked as a tattooed exotic dancer in the circus. She carved her spot into male-dominated tattoo history by opening Tattoo Emporium, her own tattoo shop, in 1939.

═══ *Fun Fact* ═══

Sailor Jerry was not some nineteenth century drunkard. His real name was Norman Collins and he was born in Reno, Nevada. Norman spent most of his days developing better tattooing methods and inks, then drawing them onto the bodies of sailors in Hawaii.

BANNED

Tattooing was banned from 1961 until 1997 in New York because of the alleged spread of hepatitis B from some Coney Island needles in the 1950s. Whether hep B was a real threat or not is debatable, but what is known for sure is that tattooing symbolized counterculture, and not everybody in the mainstream was happy about it.

Many artists picked up and relocated to more low-key Long Island, except Mike Bakaty, who just moved into a hiding space behind his East Village storefront. His shop, Fineline Tattoo, operated illegally for twenty years and is the oldest shop in Manhattan, still breaking skin to this day. After forty-six years, the ban was lifted by Mayor Rudy Giuliani when he realized that everyone was still tatting, even though it was illegal, and no new cases of hep B were being reported as a result of it.

SAILOR JERRY STYLES

Classic tattoo designs were simple but meaningful. Here are a few old-school designs that'll never go out of style.

SWALLOWS
The swallow is a homing bird, and sailors often got one of these tattooed on their shoulders after successfully navigating five thousand nautical miles. Swallows are different from sparrows, which are birds that mate for life and should be tattooed in pairs.

ANCHORS
In whatever iteration (plain or with the word *hold-fast* to ward off bad luck), anchors symbolized remaining grounded.

NAUTICAL STARS
Before Google Maps, sailors used the stars to navigate. These stars were thought of as the stars to guide them back home.

ROSE OF NO MAN'S LAND
This was a war tattoo dedicated to the nurse who mended soldiers' wounds in the field.

WOMEN
Self-explanatory.

THE MANSIONS OF NEWPORT, RHODE ISLAND

A short bus ride from Providence, over a scenic bridge that'll give you the sensation that you're flying weightless over piercing blue waters, lies a stretch of land adorned by some of 'Merica's most elegant mansions. Once inhabited by the richest people in all the land (and their European servants), these Gilded Age (aka showoff age) monster homes are a veritable collection of architectural wonders that'll make your one-bedroom feel like a cardboard box.

THE BREAKERS

A "cottage" in the grandest sense, this Italian Renaissance palazzo is the house that Vanderbilt built. Commodore Cornelius Vanderbilt made his fortune in steamships and his grandson, Cornelius Vanderbilt II, who built the mansion, was the head honcho behind the New York Central Railroad; basically, he held every railroad monopoly square on the board thereafter. Like that thousand-piece puzzle you never finished, the seventy rooms in the Breakers will make your head spin. A stable and a carriage house sit a half mile away, and whenever old Vanderbilt needed wheels, one of his twelve grooms or stable boys would hitch up the horses and roll out in style.

> ═══ *Fun Fact* ═══
>
> Not too far away, brother William Vanderbilt built the Marble House, a cold-floored wonder loaded with 500,000 cubic feet of marble.

CHATEAU-SUR-MER

A debutante's dream house, this high Victorian palatial mansion was the Gilded Age party spot, where picnics capped out at two thousand stuffy guests, and dance parties were snootily referred to as "balls." Originally owned by China trade merchant William Shepard Wetmore, after his death, Will's kids remodeled the shit out of the chateau, turning it into the elaborate Second Empire French–style monster mansion it is today.

ROSECLIFF

Built with silver-mining money, Rosecliff was owned by heiress Theresa Fair Oelrichs, who had it modeled after the Grand Trianon at Versailles, with gardens to match. If you're a fan of sweeping staircases covered in red velvet carpet and ornate chandeliers, this one's for you. The creator

Tiffany, the guy who made those "Tiffany" mosaic lamps.

of the American Beauty Rose, George Bancroft, was Rosecliff's original owner and Harry Houdini hung out here during lavish tea parties.

THE ELMS

The extensive gardens with their fountains, marble and bronze sculptures, rare plants, pavilions, and a carriage house are the appetizers to what lies inside the Elms. Built with the coal-mining fortune of Edward Julius Berwind, this mansion is filled with pieces that belong in the Louvre. The family collected priceless things like Renaissance ceramics, eighteenth-century French and Venetian paintings, and rare gemstones. Without a single white wall, every room at the Elms slaps you in the face with riches.

KINGSCOTE

This Gothic Revival mansion is a rare style in the States. It may not be as gaudy as the rest of Bellevue Avenue, but it's no mere shack, either. Kingscote, with its Hansel and Gretel charm, started the "cottage boom" and was planted in Newport in 1839. Aside from its decorative towers, windows, and porch roofs, Kingscote is notable for stained-glass work done by Louis Comfort

THE ISAAC BELL HOUSE

The Isaac Bell House's combo of styles make it the mod-est of the mansions. The best example of shingle-style architecture in the country, the house has an open Japanese floor plan, with Old English, European, and colonial American touches. Built with cotton broker money, the house is a little bleak, but unique.

OTP Tip: Visit the Green Animals Topiary Garden in nearby Portsmouth to get an eyeful of the oldest and northernmost topiary garden in the United States, with eighty different animals carved out of greenery. Edward Scissorhands couldn't have done it better.

HUNTER HOUSE

Decked out in Georgian colonial architecture, this house is all about what's inside, which is original paintings by Cosmo Alexander, Gilbert Stuart, and Robert Feke, among famous others. Colonel Wanton lived here until he fled during the American Revolution, and William Hunter, a U.S. senator and diplomat, lived here and gave it its name.

THE CHEPSTOW

The Chepstow is an Italianate-style villa with a French roof used by reclusive millionaire Edmund Schermerhorn as a summer cottage. It was passed into the hands of the Morris family, who was known for 'Merica's founding father, Robert Morris. Robert's John Hancock appears on the Declaration of Independence, the Articles of Confederation, and the Constitution. Morris's descendants lived in the antique-cluttered mansion until they gave it to the Preservation Society in 1986.

FUNKY FLEA FINDS

The cool thing about going thrift shopping in Yankee territory is the possibility of stumbling upon mid-century antiques and tchotchkes along the way. You'll still find those worn T-shirts and scuffed-up comfy boots, but digging in people's trash here sometimes turns up Americana treasures. Thrifting reveals so much about a community and its history, and these five fleas are the best places to dig for cultural gold.

BRIMFIELD ANTIQUE FLEA MARKETS, BRIMFIELD, MASSACHUSETTS

What started as a backyard sale in 1959 has now grown into a six-day summer event with over one million thrifters annually. While smaller fleas have one dedicated area, Brimfield is a full-on antiques show and spreads out across twenty-one "fields," each with its own unique offerings. This is where you go to pick up New England–specific treasures like Nantucket baskets, nautical knickknacks, and delicious lobster rolls to fuel your explorations.

GOLDEN NUGGET ANTIQUE MARKET, LAMBERTVILLE, NEW JERSEY

The Golden Nugget is full of diamonds in the rough. With a sharp eye, you'll find anything from comics to wearable threads, and other rad retro pieces. Dedicate a few hours to looking under tables and in between crevices; the vendors here have been hauling their schlocky treasures to the market every week for ages, and while it may look like chaos, they know their goods. The crates of LPs and 45s will delight your inner record geek.

BROOKLYN FLEA, BROOKLYN, NEW YORK

Nouveaux transplant Brooklynites didn't just wake up looking so stylish; it took a lot of weekend digging at the flea (and months of facial hair grooming and/or disheveling). The Brooklyn Flea has several locations in the borough and always rolls out the most diggable clothes, accessories, and crafty, locally designed goods. Whether you're in the market for a monocle or a new batch

of ironic T-shirts, loafers, or nonprescription glasses, this flea is the bee's knees.

OTP Tip: The flea is coupled with Smoargasburg in Williamsburg, where some of the best food in Brooklyn is showcased in stalls and trucks. You'll want to sample every bite and chase the whole thing with a fluffy Dough doughnut.

MOWER'S SATURDAY FLEA MARKET, WOODSTOCK, NEW YORK

Nestled in the greenery of surrounding Woodstock, Mower's happens on both Saturday and Sunday, despite its name, and is the place to go for crafty bright jewelry (some repurposed from car license plates), cool ceramics, and other collectibles. This town has been shaped by the '69 Woodstock Festival, and as such, the flea's got a bit of a hippie vibe, with free hugs, homeopathic wrinkle cream, fresh produce, and rainbow umbrellas.

ELEPHANT'S TRUNK FLEA MARKET, NEW MILFORD, CONNECTICUT

This elephant's got a lot of junk in its trunk. Merchants have been hawking tchotchkes here since the '70s, so this is the place to scoop up all those creepy, faded figurines

you remember scattered around your grandma's pad. This place is popular with "pickers," or people who make a career out of digging through rubble and flipping it for big bucks. This is one of the largest outdoor fleas in New England, so you'll probably need a wagon to haul your purchases home.

THRIFTY BONUS

FASHIONISTA VINTAGE & VARIETY, NEW HAVEN, CONNECTICUT

A fun vintage shop in a college town, this place is stuffed with glam jewelry and dresses worn by '80s prom queens. When you bring all the oddities and kooky clothes to the register, they use a clothespin to secure your new thrifty finds to the end of a stick, which you carry out of the store like Johnny Appleseed.

=== *Fun Fact* ===

Flea market does not have ironic origins. These markets started in Paris and were places where a bunch of old stuff—that was likely infested with fleas—was sold for cheap.

MOVING NEEDLE: HOW THE SEWING MACHINE CHANGED EVERYTHING

Pinning down the inventor of the first sewing machine ain't easy. In 1790, a guy in England put something together that worked, but shittily. A Frenchman then made something a little better, and a few Americans, including Elias Howe from Spencer, Massachusetts, cobbled together early sewing machines.

As everyone scrambled for patents and engaged in aggressive sales tactics to make their millions, the true origin of the first sewing machine became muddled in politics. Regardless of who did it first, the sewing machine became an important tool that not only transformed clothing into "fashion," but liberated women from the needle.

BY HAND

Life before the sewing machine relied on the patient efforts of women, sitting around and stitching clothing together and hand-making housewares. When something ripped, women would repair it. While knowing how to hand-sew is an excellent skill, sewing tied women to domesticity. The sewing machine was invented before the car and the typewriter. While at first only the rich could afford the luxury of a sewing machine, eventually, everyone got their hands on one.

SEW SUCCESSFUL

Isaac Singer improved on Howe's design, building on the Howe lock stitch (in 1846) and adding the Singer fabric feed by foot presser. Singer marketed the shit out of his machine. To compete, Howe held contests where he pinned woman against machine—and guess who always won? The fabric of life was shifting and the new possibilities made for a very efficient use of women's time. The machine punched out sturdier stitches, minimizing the need for repairs, and gave women a chance to get creative.

=== *Fun Fact* ===

Singer was as ambitious about selling his machine as he was about spreading his seed. The man fathered twenty-four children with five different women.

ACCESSIBLE FASHION

It's hard to believe, but Forever 21–type stores did not exist before the sewing machine. Tailors and seamstresses did all the heavy sewing by hand, and only the rich could afford to look haute. The spread of the sewing machine drastically cut down production times, which translated to cheaper clothing on the market. Women were now part of the workforce to some extent, operating sewing machines at textile factories. While the sewing machine gave women jobs, it made men into millionaires. Fringe products, like ruffles, frills, and ribbons, became popular as easily added embellishments to clothing.

WOMEN AS ARTISTS

Women knew how to hand-sew, but their skills were always used for utility and not quite artistry. While the sewing machine didn't free their hands to go out into the world and be the equal of men in the kind of work they did (we'll get there, eventually), it did free their hands to do artistic needlework like embroidery and embellishments, a creative expression that still inspires fashion design today. Without the machine, there would be no runway, no little black dresses, and no skinny jeans; we'd all be rocking hand-stitched potato sacks, which we can't imagine are flattering.

NYC'S LEGENDARY TREND SPOTTER

The idea of Bill Cunningham sneaking up on you from behind a halal cart and snapping a picture of your cool outfit is the dream of many a fashionista in NYC. The man has some sort of magical trend-spotting powers and has been a presence on the streets of NYC since before bell-bottoms were cool (the first time). If you see a guy who could pass for your gramps, on a bike with a camera, you'd better be wearing something awesome!

WHO'S THIS GUY?

Bill will be the first to tell you that he sucks at taking pictures. And that's just adorable, because Bill has made a long and prosperous career out of spotting, photographing, and collaging fashion trends for the *New York Times* for almost forty years. After snapping a chance photo of Greta Garbo in 1978, Bill, a Harvard dropout, started taking pictures of ordinary street people wearing extraordinary clothing. While most photographers were obsessed with celebrity fashion (which is still true today), Bill stuck to identifying the trends of regular people on the streets, and by taking money and sponsored clothing out of the equation,

he truly captured personal expression through fashion.

A 2011 documentary titled *Bill Cunningham New York* captures his everyday life. Fashion's biggest stars glam up Bill's name, but the man simply doesn't give a damn: He just rides around on his bike, stopping to snap shots of things that catch his eye, then returns to his little desk and his tiny apartment above Carnegie Hall.

HOW TO DRESS FOR BILL

Fashion-savvy New Yorkers will tell you that the thought of being caught by Bill is ever-present in the back of their mind every time they step outside. So how do you get Bill to notice you? We're sorry, but there is no method to his madness—although his madness seems to be a driver for fashion. When Bill sees an inspiring piece (or color/print/shape/texture), he collects similar fashion elements around town for a week and distills what he sees into a collage and commentary in the Sunday *New York Times*.

In this way, he not only documents trends but has a hand in actually creating them by identifying what's popular on the streets. Using the power of the press, Bill has moved the fashion world forward for decades. Will a crazy hat get Bill's attention? Maybe a stripy handbag? Who the fuck knows—but stay as close to Fifth Avenue as possible.

BUFFALO GIVES YOU WINGS

In the 1960s, it was common for trash to be turned into treasure. This was the era when the garage sale hit its stride, when people still remembered the hard times after World War II and how to make the most out of very little. Luckily for wing lovers, this was also the time when the humble chicken wing turned into really delicious bar food.

LEARN TO FLY

It's hard to imagine a time when the chicken wing was tossed out as trash or destined to be boiled into soup broth. This was just the way of the world before Teressa Bellissimo of Anchor Bar in Buffalo, New York, joined genius territory.

As legend has it, Teressa's husband Frank—who jointly founded and operated Anchor Bar—received a massive wrong order of wings instead of necks (which were used for spaghetti sauce) sometime in 1964. Rather than dump the delivery, Teressa decided to deep-fry the wings, douse them in hot sauce, and make them into dip-ready drumsticks and flats by chopping each wing into two—a revolution right up there with splitting the atom. Teressa served her invention as a gratis gift to late-night patrons at the bar, word of their awesomeness spread like wildfire, and within weeks the Buffalo chicken wing craze put the city in a choke hold.

DO THE RIGHT WING

There's no doubt that the Buffalo wing as we know and love it was invented by Bellissimo at Anchor Bar, but there will

always be naysayers who claim to have created the OG Buffalo wing. One such claim comes from John Young of Buffalo's former Wings 'N Things restaurant, who had been serving breaded chicken wings in a special mambo sauce.

Young may have been serving a hot new take on wings, but the true Buffalo name is only granted to chicken wings that meet certain criteria. The wing must be left unbreaded, split for single-handed munchability, fried, and then doused in a holy trinity blend of melted butter, hot sauce, and red pepper. The blue cheese and celery side appeared because that's all Bellissimo had available. The sauces proved necessary as perfect cooling contrasts when the heat levels got cranked up to "suicidal" or "death," current iterations of the wings you'll find at Anchor.

WINGS SPREAD

Buffalo wings have nothing to do with buffalo or bison, but everything to do with Buffalo the city in western New York. Much as Chicago's deep-dish pizza is simply referred to as pizza in Chi-town, the city of Buffalo knows its famed food as "chicken wings," or just "wings." After Anchor Bar essentially restructured the food pyramid, neighboring cities, and eventually states, caught wind of the wing craze.

One of the first to follow in Anchor's footsteps was Duff's—another Buffalo joint that has since won the local vote for its larger wings with the tagline "They started it, we perfected it." The success from such a simple recipe spawned chain restaurants like Wings 'N Curls, Hooters (which found that pairing wings with breasts was a recipe for success), and even Buffalo Wild Wings. After the Buffalo Bills football squad made four straight Super Bowl appearances, Buffalo wings became synonymous with sports and beer, which helped propel them straight up the American culinary icon ranks, right next to the almighty cheeseburger.

THE SECRETS OF NYC PIZZA

The first thing to do on everyone's bucket list in NYC is undoubtedly sample a slice of "real" pizza. Any warm-blooded American has had a slice of pizza before; we all know what it tastes like. And while it sometimes hits the spot, it's no big deal anywhere else. So what makes these pies so fucking special? Many have speculated and engaged in heavy debates about crust, sauce, water, baking temperatures, and dough-throwing techniques. Here are our two cents on the converging factors that make NYC pizza better than any other in the world (including you, Chicago!).

the hip. They know their oven's specific hot spots and have cook times down to a tee.

WATER

Is the water really better for pizza making in NYC? If whatever's living in the air can make sourdough work in San Francisco, then we suppose water can really be behind the perfect NYC pizza crust (because we all know California can't make a pizza to save it from floating into the Pacific). Now, we've sampled tap water from around the country, and we must say that New York's is by far the tastiest. Supposedly, the mineral content in the city's tap water supply adds to the texture and bubbly factor of the dough. While we're not totally convinced of that, the proof is in the pie.

OTP Tip: Don't drink the tap water in LA unless you want to develop a severe case of the shits, without a single giggle.

OVEN

Patsy Grimaldi refused to operate his now world-famous Brooklyn pizza joint in Manhattan, because the city wouldn't let him bring in his coal-fired brick oven. So, yeah, ovens matter. They're the difference between making a thin, blistered, beautiful crust and a floppy, fat one. Whether it burns coal or wood, the ovens used by New York pizza makers are attached to them at

GOLDEN RATIO

Understanding the cheese-to-sauce ratio is crucial. Too much sauce makes for a soggy crust; too much cheese, and all the flavor of both crust and sauce get overpowered by fat. The goal here is to have bits of sauce peeking through the cheese so that both can get torched by the oven, which caramelizes the seeping sauce while

flash-melting the cheese. If you want to get into a real pizza-related argument, tell a New Yorker that the cheese-to-sauce ratio isn't a factor. And make sure you have a good dental plan.

NONNA FACTOR

Nobody can deny the Italian presence in NYC. While NYC pizza and Italy have as much to do with each other as hippos and ballet, the elements of what makes a pie great stem back to the boot. Italian pizzas are all about simplicity and balance, and while American pizzas have picked up hefty toppings along the way, New Yorkers still cherish the basics, like the margherita. We're not entirely convinced that there isn't a little old Italian lady hiding behind the oven of every great pizza joint.

THE GOODS

The right way to eat NYC pizza is walking down the street, snaking through people traffic while taking bites of your pizza from a paper plate, and most $1 slice shops will do. To step up your street-walking game, grab a slice from Joe's in the West Village or John's on Bleecker. Sit down at Lombardi's—NYC's first pizza shop—just to say you did it, then hop on the train to Brooklyn. Motorino's pies are spectacular, Roberta's is a Bushwick favorite, and if you can make it out to the dead of Midwood, Di Fara's simple ingredients and perfected (i.e., slightly burnt) crust will blow your mind.

D.C.: FOOD TRUCK MECCA OF THE EAST

While 'Merica's capital is busy legislating and presiding and shit, the city streets are swarming with criminally delicious food trucks. In the land of the law, it took forever for trucks to be able to operate legally, but once food truck regulations were passed in the vendors' favor in 2013, the scene exploded. From fusion tacos to fresh handmade pasta, the awesome food in these trucks brings down the (white) house every time.

is fully customizable so you get to play your hand at fusing. To make your perfect taco, you pick a protein, slaw, sauce, and finisher (Hint: Spicy Flying Pig, #15 sauce, kimchi-lime slaw, and cheesy-lime crema), then marvel at how well Mexican flavors dance the salsa with Korean condiments.

OTP Tip: Another fusion favorite, Tako-rean's bulgogi tacos were so successful that they catapulted the truck into its first brick-and-mortar venue in 2012, with multiple locations sprouting up around the city like taco tulips.

BUT FIRST

Fojol Brothers

Operating a fleet of legendary trucks hailing from faraway places (that didn't actually exist), serving really weird food, and wearing kind of racist outfits, the Fojol Brothers were a traveling food circus. They had three trucks, each serving a different cuisine—Volothai (Thai), Merlindia (Indian), and Benethiopia (Ethiopian). They were once called hipster racists and closed their trucks in 2014 due to high operating costs. While the trucks are off the streets, founder Justin Vitarello isn't through being a weirdo, and has projects in the works. Keep an eye out for brightly colored turbans and upturned mustaches.

THE STREET FLEET

Far East Taco Grille

'Merica loves its fusion food, and D.C.'s specialty is Asian-y tacos. Far East Taco Grille

OoH Dat Chicken

Anybody with the balls to name their business OoH Dat anything deserves our attention. Who dat? Jason Mirhady, a classically trained chef from Miami, is behind this chicken—a moist, flame-kissed, dry rub-marinated rotisserie bird with OoH Dem Sides like inventive basil slaw and a coveted potato salad Jason serves only twice a week.

DC Slices

DC Slices isn't like nearby New York pizza (nobody can replicate those), but the crust is thin, they're huge, and loaded with things like buffalo chicken, blue cheese, ham, pineapple, and bubbly cheese. Get some Cajun tater tots on the side and fuggetaboutit.

Basil Thyme

A distressed silver truck that rolls out fresh dough daily, Basil Thyme makes pasta time okay anytime. You'll run your plastic fork into truffled lasagna, or pull it through melt-in-your-mouth linguine and start peeking into the truck for a nonna who made this street miracle possible. What you'll find inside is a former IT guy, and tiramisu.

Pepe

It's silver, it's sleek, and it's owned by one of the greatest chefs in the world. José Andrés's little truck serves up big jamón and manchego Spanish flavors, and while the prices are a bit steep, the flavors and creative condiments are worth it.

Pho Junkies

There are many pho trucks to choose from, but this one's got the right kind of junk in the trunk. On first approach, the truck itself is decked out in sewer colors with zombie-themed designs, and with a creature slurping up noodles on the side. The junkies make rich and hearty pho, with fatty meat cuts to which you add fresh herbs, jalapeño, and a squeeze of lime.

Red Hook Lobster Pound

Red Hook is a next-level mobile lobster shack that brings Maine to your face on the streets of D.C. Your choices here are lobster, lobster, and more lobster, on a roll, with some sauce, then down the hatch. It's $16 no matter how you cut it, but luscious chunks of lobster meat shouldn't be cheap.

Captain Cookie and the Milk Man

For a sweet finish, get a Nutella cookie and a glass of milk from the Cap'n. Huge, buttery cookies that'll make a grown man cry, make yours an ice-cream sandwich to trigger the big tears. The truck is blue, sterile, and clean, but when that sandwich starts dripping down your elbow, things will absolutely get messy.

MAINE LOBSTER LOVE SHACKS

Maine is a gorgeous state, with scenic highways, towering cliffs, picture-perfect lighthouses, and cool breezes that sweep you toward the ocean's soothing waves. But everyone knows that you don't come to Maine to fiddle around with nature. No sir! Maine is about eating your weight in lobster, in a shack, with some butter. We're not even sure anybody actually lives in Maine, other than lobsters and the people who put them on your paper plate. While the rest of the country eats lobster on white tablecloths, these lobster shacks strip down the pomp to spread the lobstah love.

YOUNG'S LOBSTER POUND, BELFAST, MAINE

While you can get a pound of lobster, the name actually refers to a lobster pound, like an aquatic dog pound, but with lobster instead of canines. Not only is the lobster here fantastic and you can scarf it down on the docks, but Young's lets you BYOB, which makes for a dangerous situation. Being beer-drunk with so much good lobster around will leave you penniless.

BAGADUCE LUNCH, BROOKSVILLE, MAINE

Bagaduce sits on a tidal river, and the moment you get your lobster roll, the birds will circle overhead. It will be you against them, so protect your roll by eating it as fast as possible. This walk-up window shack earned a coveted James Beard Award and, aside from lobster, the haddock burgers here are fantastic. Fuck it, bag a tres in here.

THE CLAM SHACK, KENNEBUNK, MAINE

Don't let the cheating name fool you: The Clam Shack is full of great lobster. In the land of lobster, every little thing you can do to set your shack apart matters. Here, the owner insists on only using his hands to break apart the lobster meat, because he says knives bruise the meat and cause oxidation. The meat is served warm on a homemade roll, with both mayo and butter for a gluttonous creaminess you won't be able to resist. We're not sure the science behind this checks out, but our mouths tell us he might be onto something.

MCLOONS LOBSTER SHACK, SOUTH THOMASTON, MAINE

Like something straight outta *SpongeBob SquarePants*, this red shack will serve you a crabby patty (in cake or sandwich form) if you want it, but we're here for lobster rolls, so shush. McLoons doesn't mess around: Its roll is so overflowing with tender tail and claw meat that you'll have trouble keeping it from escaping the corners of your mouth. Plus, the view outside is unbeatable, with islands, boats, and buoys arranged like a postcard from paradise.

WATERMAN'S BEACH LOBSTER, SOUTH THOMASTON, MAINE

Offering dining in the lobster's very own back/frontyard, this spruced-up shack sits near a wooden dock with a saltwater farm. The lobster here gets a sauna steam over saltwater that imparts just the right amount of briny ocean tang, and instead of a split-top roll, the meat is evenly spread on a burger bun.

OTP Tip: If you're here in August, hit the Maine Lobster Festival in Rockland. You'll need a bib and a healthy appetite.

SCARBOROUGH FISH & LOBSTER, SCARBOROUGH, MAINE

The cheapest roll on this list, this one's only $10 for a quarter pound of meat, lightly tossed in mayo with a healthy sprinkle of paprika on top. Settle into Scarborough's wooden picnic area, and savor the simple perfection of the best deal in Maine.

IT'S SHOWTIME!

You can ride the subway to get to music, but there's all kinds of music hidden right on the platforms. Public performance is deeply entrenched in the New York City ethos. Whether you want to or not, your ears will be filled with sounds, your eyes distracted with dance, and your body sometimes caught in the performance cross fire. Here's a handful of shows you'll likely see if you put your ear to the underground.

WEST 4TH

This multilevel platform has trains rushing into it from all sides, unless it's 2 a.m. on a Saturday; then you're sitting there hoping to stay awake long enough to make it home. A smelly mecca of sounds, depending on the day, you can hear anything from the rolling beats of guys playing plastic trash

cans to a traveling doo wop group, to a guy blowing a little too hard into a sax.

14TH STREET F/M

The tunes here are of the singer/songwriter variety. Look for a single lady with a guitar, belting out love songs, or a Mexican dude strumming along solemnly. If you're not in a hurry, the trains come frequently enough that you can sit down on the bench, listen to an entire song, and contract a case of the feels.

METROPOLITAN L

The L train platform is where your room-mate disappears with his keyboard and harmonica late at night. Things get really experimental down here; sometimes a guy will rap in sync with a guitar player across the platform; other times a twangy goth princess will do her rendition of Gaga. It's really a mixed bag of weird, occasionally great, performances.

A TRAIN

Riding the A train between Manhattan and Brooklyn is your best bet to catch the famous break/pole dancers who flip around the car to Michael Jackson classics. When you hear, "It's showtime!" tuck your appendages close to your body, because shit's about to get wild.

UNION SQUARE

Music Under New York was started in 1985, and puts on more organized shows daily for commuters. While the program operates in many stations, the Union Square location—from heavy metal bands to country singers—has the best acts. It's easy to get caught up in the music, but keep your wits about you; this is a major intersection of tourists, worker bees, and other fast-moving New Yorkers. Stopping to smell the roses here might get you trampled.

THE (KIND OF SHADY) LEGEND OF WOODSTOCK

Any good old hippie has a soft spot for (and maybe from) Woodstock of '69, the now legendary festival that makes every other hippie-fest pale in comparison. It may come as a surprise that there were zero "peace and love" ideals behind the event, even though the thoughts of the day leaned that way.

As it turns out, Woodstock left huge holes in the money-grubbin' pockets of the guys behind it. Many have tried to re-create the fest for years after '69, but to no avail. This is the sort of shady story behind the most iconic music festival in America.

THE BIG IDEA

While Woodstock was very much about sex, drugs, rock 'n' roll, and free love, the festival's original purpose was an opportunity for rich dudes to invest their money to make more money. Organized by get-rich-quick-minded twenty-year-olds John Roberts, Joel Rosenman, Artie Kornfeld, and Mike Lang, tickets were printed for $7 (one day), $13 (two days), and $18 (the full three days), and when scouting potential venues, the guys claimed no more than 50,000 festgoers would attend. They actually hoped for over 250,000 revelers, but it was hard to convince landowners to allow a bunch of teenage, music-lovin' zombies onto their property, so the numbers were fudged down a bit (a lot,

actually). A venue in Wallkill was secured with these bullshittin' tactics, but it fell through at the last minute and the guys began crapping their pants.

THE BIGGER TURNOUT

After some initial doubt, a dairy farm in Bethel agreed to host the event, and the party was back on. A few days before the August 15th event, a load of overachiever hippies showed up and set up camp around the venue, which wasn't fully secured and ready for orderly ticket ripping. The organizers had no choice but to turn the now hippie-invaded event into a free concert.

Word spread, and half a million others showed up. To understand the scale of this thing, the event caused the city of Bethel to become the third largest municipality in New York state for the weekend. People left their cars on the road because of the traffic, and everyone was trapped. Performers were flown in by helicopter, as was food, something the fest planners ran out of before the first musician hit the stage, and sandwiches were later donated by just-as-trapped locals.

THE MUDDY MUSIC

The festival ended up rolling over for four full days; three people died (one from a heroin overdose, another from a burst

appendix, and the last one was run over by a fucking tractor). Nobody could poop in the proper places because porta-potties were limited and it started to rain, the mud becoming the perfect cover-up for legit filth. But none of it mattered much because the music (and drugs) moved people.

When Janis Joplin, the Grateful Dead, and Creedence Clearwater Revival took the stage, the magic negated the mud and the now legendary closing performance by Jimi Hendrix—complete with a guitar solo of "The Star-Spangled Banner"—made for an unforgettable fest. Woodstock '69 is no more, but will forever live on in the acid-burned minds of many an aging hippie.

WHO GIVES A FOLK?

Folk music is all-American, and when we think about it, our minds might wander to a toothless man plucking away at his banjo somewhere deep in the South. But the Yankees put up a formidable folk game, and throw hollerin' hootenannies to prove it. Throw your banjo over your shoulder and feel the folking tunes at these fests.

NEWPORT FOLK FESTIVAL, RHODE ISLAND (LAST WEEKEND OF JULY)

The best way to get to Newport is to hop on a city bus from Providence. After about an hour of uneventful bus riding, the trees give way to blue ocean, dotted with sailboats, and Newport appears in the distance across a narrow bridge. The bus drops you off within walking distance of the festival and you'd better be ready to get folking. This little city is filled with retiree vacationers and art school students, and, come folk time, everyone commingles in a shweaty, uke-loving mess, welcoming mainlanders with open, unshaved arm(pit)s. The acts are current and popular (like Iron & Wine), with a few old-school favorites thrown in for the gray crowd.

LOWELL FOLK FESTIVAL, MASSACHUSETTS (LAST WEEKEND OF JULY)

Chances are you've never been to (or ever heard of) Lowell. It's usually good for dive bars and bundles of garbage blowing in the wind. But come the end of July, Lowell's downtown cleans up to welcome the fest, which is partly folk, with random international styles hijacking the sound waves as well. While it may not be all folk, it's always free. You can wander for three days, munching on varied international cuisine, kickin' up trash while listening to the sweet, eclectic sounds emanating from the festival's five stages. Just don't stay until Monday, when postfest trash mingles with the preexisting conditions to create something less thumpy and a lot more dumpy.

TWO FOLK FESTS, NEW YORK

When you're in New York, you never have to choose just one thing. Have pastrami on your pizza, your cheesecake with a side of hot dogs, and your folk two ways. Folk is naked without beards, and the beard-to-bare ratio at both of these fests is quite high.

Big Daddy Folk, Clearwater's Great Hudson River Revival (Late June)

It all started in the '60s with Pete Seeger, who wanted to clean up the filthy Hudson River by raising funds to build a symbolic sailboat through folk performances. People came to see Seeger sing, ride the sailboat, and contribute to his mission to de-gunk the Hudson. The festival gained a lot of steam and is a huge event on the river at Croton-on-Hudson, where you can eat, drink, and live (camp) all weekend with artists like Ani DiFranco playing in the background.

Little Hip Folk, Brooklyn Folk Fest (Mid-April)

The Jalopy is a little music school and performance space in Red Hook, Brooklyn. It operates year-round, putting on eclectic performances that range from Brooklyn bluegrass to funked-up gospel. Once a

year, the best folks get together for the fest and rage until the fiddle strings snap.

The seating is church pews and the lyrics are usually vulgar. Keep an eye on Jerron Paxton, who gets down and real dirty and says the darndest things, and watch Jackson Lynch play that fiddle like he's twenty-five going on seventy.

OTP Tip: Follow the acts to the adjacent bar to get really folked up after the show!

ROOTS ON THE RAILS, EVERYWHERE (ALL THE TIME)

If you like your folk on wheels, Roots on the Rails is the ultimate party train. In operation since 2003, each trip is unique and includes a sleeper seat, wine, beer, meals, and snacks, and, most important, a never-ending music party in the performance car. You also get access to ground shows featuring the performers onboard at the destination. Trips differ in length and route, sometimes bringing the ruckus to the glacial quiet of Anchorage, Alaska, other times disturbing the peace along the California coast. In 2014, they kept the party going for eight straight days from NYC to LA. Folk on a train is bound to beat snakes on a plane any day.

SEX *and* PARTYING

BOSTON'S BRO-IEST BEER BARS

Boston and its surrounding areas are the epitome of college towns just because there are so many there. We're not naming Boston's bro-iest bars for the sake of alliteration alone; the place is swarming with basic bros. Whether you choose to use this list as a guide to which places you'll scout out for your most lasting bromances, or as a blacklist of places to avoid on the weekends, these bars bring out the best bros in Boston.

CLERYS

Clerys has been all bro-ed out since the first bro emerged from the womb. It attracts bros from far and wide, including fans of the Georgia Bulldogs and the Washington Redskins. Clerys has games blaring on its screens and several areas where bros eat wings, hug other bros, and dance to old-school hip-hop with potential one-night stands in typical bro fashion.

POUR HOUSE

On bro-y Boylston Street, the Pour House delivers what it promises: extra-strong pours in extra-large drinks. If you weren't very bro-y to begin with, this bar makes sure to add enough liquid fuel to get you from zero to asshole in one drink flat. The dank basement, where games are frequently on the TV, also differentiates this bro bar from the rest of the strip.

PATRON'S

Foosball is a bro-magnet, and evidence of bros' patronage is ever-present with red Solo cups all over this joint. The beer here flows cheap and the eats are Mexican-inspired (gringo baby back ribs, bro!). Patron's is the kind of place where you wear a sports sweatshirt even if you don't play anything or support any team.

WHITE HORSE TAVERN

You know that raunchy smell of a bar at 10 a.m. when you have to go recover your credit card the next day? While we don't normally notice it during peak bar hours (the beer inside us probably cancels out the smell of floor beer), White Horse breaks that rule. You smell it before you see it, and the bros are solely responsible for making this thing a pit of sweat and other stanky smells.

DILLONS

The only thing you need to know about Dillons is that you'll be swimming through a sea of popped collars and vodka Red Bulls. When the weather's right, the wooden picnic tables on the outdoor patio are the perfect place to build new bromances over tater tots with sriracha dipping sauce.

TAVERN IN THE SQUARE

Tavern in the Square is game-day central. The most common thing you'll hear in here is this: "Get da fuck away from da bah. We need shats before da game comes on." If the Red Sox, Bruins, Celtics, or anything involving a ball, bat, or puck is on, you'd better get your brewskies in order: Shit's about to get wild.

MARY ANN'S (AKA SCARY ANN'S)

Whenever a place gets a nickname from the regulars, it becomes a local institution, and this one has the word *scary* attached to it permanently. The place has questionable cleanliness standards, and no windows, which means you'll be trapped in a bro-ing boiler room with $2 beers and little chance of escaping sober or dry. According to Ann's posted sign, "The beer is warm, flat, and expensive—if you're not careful, you end up wearing as much as you drink."

CRASHING IVY LEAGUE PARTIES

Who can join this league of Ivy? It's reserved for the crème de la crème; the young, sexy-ish, rarely broke, and (only sometimes) smart. But just because you're banned from class doesn't mean you can't party with the best of 'em. These five Ivy League schools were started long ago, by people in wigs, and you must respect the order of the elite by, at the very least, memorizing their mottos, even when you're getting shitfaced and crashing their favorite parties.

HARVARD, CAMBRIDGE, MASSACHUSETTS

Motto: Veritas

Veritas means "truth" and you must lie and cheat to get to the illuminati goods here. Take the Harvard Tour that is led by current students. For $10, you can check out old buildings and slyly get the inside scoop on the after-party. One way or another, you'll likely end up at Hong Kong in Harvard Square (affectionately known as the "Kong," but we've heard "Dong," too). You'll only need to stick to your "I'm just checking out the school for next year" backstory for ten minutes; the Scorpion Bowls, a two-person jungle juice thing with tiny plastic animals that'll saw your brain in half, will take over thereafter.

YALE, NEW HAVEN, CONNECTICUT

Motto: Lux et veritas

Yale is known for (and students actually going to) campuswide theme parties, and Toad's Place is where to go for intel. Dorm parties lean toward wine, cheese, and sitting around shining the light (*lux*) on the truth (*veritas*). But come game time, Yalies pull out all the snobby stops and get shitty, loud, and obnoxious. Embrace the bulldog as your spirit animal and you should do just fine.

DARTMOUTH, HANOVER, NEW HAMPSHIRE

Motto: Vox clamantis in deserto

At Dartmouth, you will find mighty fine frat basements, so you'd better learn how to play beer pong HARD. Hanover is in no way a party town and everyone goes to bed at 10 p.m. *You will be the voice of one crying out in the wilderness* (their kooky motto), because, for fuck's sake, how did you end up in a basement in New Hampshire?

COLUMBIA, NEW YORK, NEW YORK

Motto: In lumine tuo videbimus lumen

Located in upper Manhattan, Columbia's campus is well-positioned to absorb you into NYC's madness. Weekend subway service is terrible, so start the party on Thursday and pony up for cab fare to the Lower East Side where you'll have to get your new Columbia friends to stop flashing their Ivy League cards. On the weekends, rub elbows with NYU-ers at 1020, a bar close enough to campus that your cab fare won't equal the school's tuition. *In thy 6 a.m. light we see light* is their motto, or something like that.

UPENN, PHILADELPHIA, PENNSYLVANIA

Motto: *Leges sine moribus vanae*

When *Playboy* says something, we listen. Back in 2014, *Playboy* named UPenn the top party school in the nation (take that, topless coeds across schools in the Midwest!). What earned them this high honor?

UPenn's frat boys are hard-hitting, underground monster party animals and will stop at nothing to topple a keg, spring the shit out of spring break, and spend more money on liquor for parties than the townies make in a year. The school's motto is *Life without morals is useless*; morals likely showed up to UPenn's party and got useless in no time.

COCKTAILS OF THE EAST

American drinking habits (and drink mixing) began in the East. While the origin of the word *cocktail* is hotly (and likely, drunkenly) disputed, it is said that its first utterance was in New York. To us, it matters little where it came from. What matters to us is that it's good and strong. Here are some regionally specific drinks that you need to down in their home states.

APPLEJACK (APPLEJACK BRANDY + LEMON JUICE + GRENADINE), NEW JERSEY

The Garden State is known for producing mighty fine tomatoes, but Jersey also grows delicious apples in its many orchards. But while the rest of 'Merica was eating their apples out of hand, Jersey began fermenting apple juice into the strongest, mouth-puckering cider you can imagine. At 30 to 40 percent alcohol content, Applejack is a concentrated spirit and was first made in America's oldest distillery, Laird & Company, which has been continuously producing the strong stuff since 1780.

=== *Fun Fact* ===

During the colonial period, Applejack was used as currency to pay road construction crews. Shocking! Who could have guessed that America's roads were built by drunks?

CAPE CODDER (VODKA + CRANBERRY JUICE), MASSACHUSETTS

Known as a cranberry vodka to the wannabe detoxing-while-partying crowd, the Cape Codder came to be with a big push in 1945 from Ocean Spray, whose cranberry company was formed in Hanson, Massachusetts, in 1930. How do you get people to drink more of your cranberry juice? Pair it with booze and give it a fancy name, that's how.

THE OLD VERMONT (GIN + MAPLE SYRUP + LEMON JUICE + ORANGE JUICE + BITTERS), VERMONT

Maple syrup is the lifeblood of Vermont and it's not surprising that it drips into everything, including cocktails. The important thing here is Bar Hill Gin, a very fragrant, juniper-forward gin that balances the maple syrup in this cozy cocktail. Bobby Flay messed around with this and made his version with whateverthefuck gin.

THE SPREE (BEER + WINE + LIQUOR), NEW HAMPSHIRE

Alcohol taxes vary from state to state (in Washington state, for instance, the tax is over $35 per gallon). New Hampshire, on the other hand, has the lowest liquor tax in the nation at pennies per gallon. So buy bottles, buy kegs, buy vodka luges if you want. We're too drunk here to name a cocktail. But know that last call is 1 a.m., and you've gotta get to the store before 11:45 p.m.

THE SOMBRERO (ALLEN'S COFFEE FLAVORED BRANDY + MILK), MAINE

If Maine could stick a lobster in its cocktails it would—and it does! If you're willing to shelve out $29, the Bloody Mary at the Brant Point Grill is topped with a quarter pound lobster tail! But at the far other end of the spectrum, the Sombrero is a cheap, sweet concoction that's had Maine by the balls for years. The key ingredient is Allen's Coffee Flavored Brandy, served with milk in a highball glass. It's sugary, 60 proof, and loaded with caffeine, which explains its wonderful nicknames, including the Downeast Panty Remover, Bitch Whiskey, Fatass in a Glass, and Trailer Park Toddy, among others.

=== *Fun Fact* ===

One out of eight bottles of booze purchased in Maine is Allen's.

THE BRONX (GIN + VERMOUTH + ORANGE JUICE; SHAKEN), PENNSYLVANIA

The Bronx was (allegedly) created in Philly by Joseph S. Sormani, a guy from the Bronx. It's essentially a gin martini with orange juice and was the first drink that Alcoholics Anonymous founder Bill Wilson remembers drinking during World War I, which is saying something. The sweet orange takes the martini edge off, and if you're looking to get addicted to booze, this is the way to go (with a cheesesteak in the other hand).

THE RICKEY (GIN OR BOURBON + LIME + CLUB SODA), WASHINGTON, D.C.

The Rickey is one old drink with its bourbon roots firmly planted in the nation's capital since 1880. While current variations are made with a hit of gin (or sometimes completely without booze, which is just fizzy lime water), the older version of the cocktail calls for a "wineglass full of gin." Colonel Joe Rickey, a Democratic lobbyist, was a morning drinker at Shoomaker's and he liked his bourbon iced. One day, the bartender threw in a lime to wake Rickey the fuck up, and the cocktail has kept a following on the Hill since.

READER'S CHOICE (SOMETHING OLD + SOMETHING NEW + SOMETHING BORROWED + SOMETHING BLUE), NEW YORK

We hope you understand how hard it is to pick a drink to represent the drinkiest town in America. You could go for the obvious Manhattan, the classic blend of rye, sweet vermouth, and bitters, or its many modern riffs, like the Red Hook and Carroll Gardens. Maybe take a shot at getting a Brooklyn, a rarely made drink that uses ingredients that pretty much dried up during Prohibition. What about a Moscow Mule? Its spicy ginger beer notes call to us daily. Or just throw all caution to the wind, pick up a Long Island Iced Tea (pretty much five drinks in one), and we'll see you on the subway at 6 a.m., asleep and inexplicably on your way to Coney Island.

MIDDLE 'MERICA

The Midwest is the farming heartland of America, but it's not all tractors and sacks of potatoes (well, not all of it). Midwesterners love their sports, including monster trucks and the Super Bowl, and the people here are deathly nice; like, so nice that you may think they're all robots and you might start looking for their switches. Despite being raised on tater tots and Olive Garden, some seriously talented people, like architect Frank Lloyd Wright and our favorite drummer, Dave Grohl, hail from the Midwest. Throw on some Motown jams and let the cheese in Wisconsin melt your soul.

THE ULTIMATE GREAT LAKES ADVENTURE

Your hands and feet will look like Grandma's for a week after you're done with this adventure. There are so many lakes, here: The main five and a bunch on islands, plus so many caves, dunes, and water parks around them that you'll swear you're turning amphibious. Get one foot in Canada and one in the United States and prepare for the grandest Great Lakes adventure of all time.

LAKE SUPERIOR

With over 10,000 paddle-able individual lakes, Superior's waters poke through the border of Wisconsin and Minnesota, and create some cold, cold diving opportunities. If you can handle the blood-chilling cold of the Apostle Islands National Lakeshore, you'll be treated to underwater wonders like rare rock formations and shipwrecks that'll make the *Titanic* look like a tugboat.

The Smith Moore Wooden Steam Barge is the most popular wreck, sitting ninety feet in the water, perfectly preserved from its catastrophic collision back in 1889. For more frigid fun, the waterfalls freeze over in a kaleidoscope of dangerous icicles, sea caves become cold, chambers echo, and pillar ice bridges form between islands. For something more summery, the Noah's Ark Water Park at the Wisconsin Dells is the largest in the country, with fifty-one slides like the Black Anaconda, a combo of slide and roller coaster.

=== *Fun Fact* ===

The Washington Island Stave Church (called Stavkirke) looks like a Nordic haunted house in the forest. It is a rare example of a Scandinavian wood and stone church from the Middle Ages.

LAKE MICHIGAN

Lake Michigan is the aquatic escape for landlocked Midwesterners and its shores are populated with the pastiest population in all the land. You, too, can come here for the boats and watersports, but the biggest thrill is the sand dunes. While there are many peaceful dunes where you can relax and get sandy, to kick up some dirt go to the Silver Lake State Park and frolic around two thousand acres of moving dunes. You can rent a buggy or bring your own sand-action vehicle. Ludington State Park, with its beautiful shoreline and charming lighthouse, is the perfect place to camp when you've duned your last dune.

=== *Fun Fact* ===

Fulgurites, or formations made when the intense heat of lightning strikes and melts sand, can be found all over the shores of Lake Michigan.

LAKE ERIE

A two-hour drive from the Pitts(burgh), you'll find blue waters and sandy beaches at Presque Isle Park, where you can play as much sand volleyball as your lake-lovin' soul desires. The big adventure here, though, is indoors. The Splash Lagoon Indoor Water Park Resort boasts the East's largest indoor wave pool, with 200,000 gallons of pissed-in paradise. You can also play laser tag, arcades, or float belly-up in the lazy river. Drier thrills can be found at the Waldameer Park and Water World, a 120-year-old park with rickety wooden coasters that'll rattle your bones.

LAKE HURON

Manitoulin Island, the largest freshwater lake island in the world, stands in the middle of Lake Huron. There's a lake inside the island (this is some meta shit, Earth!), and a fun thing to do is the Cup and Saucer Trail (which proves that the closer you get to Canada, the cuter the names of things become). On a 7.5-mile hiking trail, you'll traverse 4–mile cliffs, quarries, and challenging climbs, and tiptoe around some seriously scenic land.

LAKE ONTARIO

The most popular attraction here is Niagara Falls, but once you've worn out your blue poncho, head to Toronto on the Canadian side of Lake Ontario. The city sits right on the lake, and kayaking, canoeing, and paddleboarding is a way of life. Seafaring through the Beaver River is a four-hour scenic float, while navigating Algonquin's Ragged Falls will throw you around a bit. The best thing to do here is the paddle-in concerts held at the Molson Amphitheatre, an outdoor venue where your kayak serves as stadium seating while you watch the likes of the Foo Fighters and Zeppelin tribute bands.

MONSTER TRUCK JAM

The Monster Truck Jam is what happens when you dream of playing with toy cars on a grand scale. A worldwide spectacle, the Monster Truck Jam is WrestleMania on wheels and rolls into Ford Field in car country, Detroit, every February, bringing with it the most ridiculous of trucks and the absurd fans who love 'em.

THAT'S THE JAM

Depending on the venue, the trucks either race each other or go at it in a freestyle competition. We prefer the race format for faster cars (like the Indy 500), and, luckily, Ford Field normally hosts the freestyle version of the jam. The goal here is to get as many ridiculous tricks under your wheels as you can in ninety seconds (plus a thirty-second bonus). Truck tricks include doughnuts, crushing cars, breaking through barriers, getting air on ramps, and goddamn backflips! While the event is a circus of trucks that travels worldwide, its St. Louis origin makes it an event the Midwest gets behind 100 percent.

TRUCK MONSTERS

While we will never understand why grown men get out of bed, put on their "Made in 'Merica" T-shirts, complete with bald eagles, flags, and Uncle Sams, and pony up the hundreds of dollars for admission to watch a tricked-out truck crush cars, we accept that it happens, and that it will likely never die. Here are a few of the key frankentrucks to know so that you, too, can get down with the most cockamamie car event in this country.

BIGFOOT

This was the first monster ever built; Bob Chandler put this beast together in St. Louis in the mid-'70s. Chandler was a shitty driver and kept modifying his Ford F-250 every time he broke it, until its wheels were sixty-six inches high and it could crush everything in sight. Eighteen versions of Bigfoot have been made to date.

GRAVE DIGGER

A morbid incarnation of creator Dennis Anderson's phrase, "I'll take this old junk and dig you a grave with it," the truck is a puke-green legend with mighty wheels and a huge fan base. At any given time, there are nine of these bad boys on the track around the country to keep enthusiasm running high.

THE RAMINATOR

If trucks were people (and to some people they are), the Raminator would be Bigfoot's biggest enemy. This truck rammed Bigfoot out of its big winning streak back in early 2000 and has been a feared competitor ever since.

AFTERSHOCK

A souped up Chevy, this thing flew over a school bus in Toronto and made all the spectators pee their pants just a little.

BULLDOZER

With a name like *Bulldozer*, you can probably guess that this guy crushes shit with gusto. And you'd be right. Plus it has one of the first 3-D body shells and horns protruding from its roof.

MCGRUFF THE CRIME-PREVENTION DOG

Around since the '70s, this one's for the kids. McGruff the crime-prevention dog was reincarnated as a truck in 1996. Back then, the whole truck was a dog body, but it was changed later to be more streamlined. Its owner teamed up with the National Crime Prevention Council to teach kids that, when it comes to crime, it's best to put down the gun and hop in a giant truck and destroy shit instead.

Follow these rules closely at the Monster Truck Jam, or risk sticking out like one of the reasonable humans. Who are absolutely not welcome here.

1. You must be drunk. There is no justifying this unless you're drunk.

2. You must develop a deep love of seeing things crushed.

3. You must embrace saying things in triplicates: SUNDAY! SUNDAY! SUNDAY!

4. Your outfit must feature flames.

5. The mullet: If you want to do it right, make sure the party in the back is ratty and long enough to drape down a window, like Rapunzel.

OTP Tip: Stop by the Henry Ford Museum in Dearborn, Michigan, to pay tribute to the man who (unintentionally) made the Monster Truck Jam possible. Here, you'll find a jar containing Ford's last breath, the limo Kennedy was assassinated in, and the bloody chair in which Lincoln was shot.

THE WORLD'S LARGEST TREASURE HUNT

The Midwest is speckled with some really weird shit that's the "world's largest" by default, mostly because nobody else is going to sit around constructing a bigger ball of twine. We're going on an adventure to hunt down each one of these big-ass oddities.

WORLD'S LARGEST BASKET BUILDING, NEWARK, OHIO

How'd you like to go to work in a nine-thousand-ton, seven-story basket? Well, the five hundred employees at the Long-aberger Company have been bobbing and weaving here since 1997. The building was modeled after the company's best-selling basket, there's a huge atrium inside, and the handles are heated during icy weather to keep them from breaking. At one time, baskets were the equivalent of paper bags. Now, it's just super-weird for a huge basket to sit off Route 16.

WORLD'S LARGEST MUSKIE, HAYWARD, WISCONSIN

What the fuck's a muskie, you ask? Its formal black-tie name is *muskellunge*, and it's a relatively rare freshwater fish that's long as an eel and strong as a bull. It's part of the pike family, and its name means "ugly pike"—but that didn't stop the good people

of Hayward from constructing a four-story, city block–long version of it. The world's largest fiberglass sculpture, you'll find this fish sticking out of the land in the National Fresh Water Fishing Hall of Fame, with fishing exhibits in its belly and an observation deck shooting out of its toothy mouth.

WORLD'S LARGEST KETCHUP BOTTLE, COLLINSVILLE, ILLINOIS

It makes perfect sense for America's favorite condiment to have a giant statue erected in its honor. After all, how else are we going

to push the obnoxious envelope with foreigners who have real sauces? Now, this isn't just some run-of-the-mill ketchup; it's "Catsup," Brooks Old Original Tangy Catsup, to be exact. A 170-foot-tall water tower, this monster bottle was created in 1949 by the company as a pat on the back for being the most popular condiment around. This one's high up on stilts, presumably to keep the French from defacing it.

WORLD'S LARGEST BALL OF TWINE, CAWKER CITY, KANSAS

Like a cat toy for the world's largest feline, this ball of twine is constructed from seven million feet of sisal twine. If unrolled, the twine would stretch approximately from Cawker City to New York. At a forty-foot circumference, the ball was started by Frank Stober in 1953 for reasons unknown. Follow the painted path and add your own twine during the twine-a-thon in August.

WORLD'S LARGEST JOLLY GREEN GIANT, BLUE EARTH, MINNESOTA

In 1979, Paul Hedberg—a radio DJ who interviewed people passing through town—was so hell-bent on canned vegetables that he gave them out to guests at the end of his show. The construction of Interstate-90, which would bypass the town, threatened Paul's supply of show guests, so he needed to make some bold moves. Using mostly his own money (who the hell was paying him enough to construct a ridiculous statue?), Paul erected this towering Green Giant, a 55.5-foot-tall man, with size 78 shoes, who wears a leafy toga.

OTP Tip: Go for the Giant and stay for the museum, dedicated to the man in green, and featuring all kinds of veggie memorabilia.

BONUS

HUMONGOUS FUNGUS

Every year, Crystal Falls, Michigan, celebrates a giant patch of mushrooms. The 1,500-year-old Armillaria gallica, which is a glorified button mushroom that mostly grows underground, is a disappointing sight, but the festival features three days of pancake breakfasts, tournaments, and a ten-square-foot mushroom pizza.

AMERICA'S BEST ROLLER COASTERS

While the Russians (or the French, depending on who you ask) are credited with creating the first coasters, the American thrill game is strong. Americans are quite interested in how far they can push it before they die (which, given the amount of accidents at the rolling hands of coasters, isn't an exact science).

The beginning of the American coaster is the wooden, rickety Cyclone (not the first, but the most popular) that's still in operation at Coney Island. Its popularity got the gears turning for new designs, using different materials and manipulations of kinetic energy. Today, the country is covered with monster coasters that'll turn your belly butterflies into a flock of seagulls.

GOLIATH, SIX FLAGS GREAT AMERICA, GURNEE, ILLINOIS

Even before anything particularly scary happens, the first lift is tilted up so steeply (45 degrees) that you know shit's going to get wild. Once you're hauled to the top of this giant, prepare to lose your lunch as the ride twists and drops you like a rag doll. While the coaster is 165 feet tall, the big drop totals 180 feet, which means you go through the ground for 15 feet into a tunnel. Plus, you don't even have the security of steel to calm your jittery nerves because this thing is mostly wood, which guarantees whiplash.

> === *Fun Fact* ===
>
> The first Six Flags opened in Arlington, Texas, and was called "Six Flags over Texas" because of the state's historical colonization, which saw six actual flag changes, namely from Spain, France, Mexico, the Republic of Texas, the USA, and the Confederate States of America.

STEEL HAWG, INDIANA BEACH, MONTICELLO, INDIANA

We love going high and fast, but there is something about a ridiculous drop angle that churns our stomachs. At 111 degrees, the Steel Hawg has the steepest vertical drop in the United States. That means you're not dropping straight down, but at a curve, fucking backward.

MILLENNIUM FORCE, CEDAR POINT, SANDUSKY, OHIO

At 6,595 feet, the tracks of Millennium Force are super-long, but the whole ride takes a mere two minutes and twenty seconds from gripping start to face-numbing finish. How do you get through that much track in that short a time? Go fast, 93 MPH to be exact. While this isn't the fastest ride in the United States, consistently flying through the air for way longer than you'd ever want makes this the most nauseating. You may want to jump ship after a few seconds, but the only way out is to ride the pony all the way to the end.

OTP Tip: If you need more speed with less dicking around, the Top Thrill Dragster at this park reaches an eyeball-gripping 120 MPH.

KINGDA KA, SIX FLAGS GREAT ADVENTURE, JACKSON, NEW JERSEY

The current highest roller coaster in the world, at 456 feet (and the fastest in the United States at 128 MPH), this thing needs a hydraulic push to even make it up that high and fuck-ups are basically built into the ride. The ride is under a minute, but it's an adrenaline rush like no other. It plays with the human psyche, injecting fear through anticipation (and sometimes malfunction). If you fear heights even a little, Kingda Ka is your worst nightmare.

ART *and* DESIGN

FOLLOW THE POPEYE TRAIL

No amount of CrossFit will ever give you the kind of mallet forearms Popeye got from spinach. The one-eyed slurry sailor is a classic American cartoon character who embodied that on-the-seas worker era, with a fair sprinkling of racism. Popeye is as American as diabetes, and one park in Illinois makes sure that the sailorman will never die.

ALL EYES ON POPEYE

Why did people love this guy so much? Well, there was all the racism against the Japanese during World War II and soldiers needed a good justification for being in the line of fire. Additionally, Popeye was created during the Depression, and reminded people of better times. Story lines of holding onto your love (even if she treats you like garbage), friendship (even if he steals ya girl), and how it's okay to be a dumb, old drunk fared well with the down-and-out audience. Plus, Wimpy loved his hamburgers and so did America.

=== *Fun Fact* ===

During the height of Popeye's popularity, sales of spinach rose 33 percent and it became wildly popular, especially among kids. Allen's Popeye brand spinach is still the second-largest-selling brand in America.

SCULPTURE TRAIL

Popeye came to life in Thimble Theatre, a comic strip about the Oyl family that was created in 1919. Castor Oyl (Olive's brother) needed a sailor and picked up the one-eyed Popeye in 1929. The rest of the gang was created along the way, until the crew took on a life of their own. While Popeye has long sailed into the sunset, sculptures of the show's characters are continually being erected in Chester, Illinois, the hometown of the cartoon's creator, Elzie Crisler (E. C.) Segar.

The main organizer is the town undertaker, so every new statue is carved from a solid block of granite, like a cartoony tombstone. While a Popeye statue has stood in Chester since 1977, the town started unveiling new characters at its annual Popeye picnic, starting with Wimpy, in 2006, with plans to erect one per year until 2020. Here's a breakdown of notable statues you'll find around town.

Popeye (1977), Chester Bridge

He is what he is, and what he is is a six-foot-tall, nine-hundred-pound bronze statue erected by sorority girls.

J. Wellington Wimpy (2006), Gazebo Park

Known for his penchant for burgers and

conning people for coins, Wimpy was Popeye's lazy friend and the inspiration behind an actual burger joint in the UK.

Olive Oyl, Swee'Pea, and Eugene the Jeep (2007), Randolph County Courthouse

Popeye loved lanky Olive Oyl, and at some point, Swee'Pea, a baby who could pack a punch; she arrived on Popeye's doorstep (presumably because, back then, cartoons being knocked up was not okay). Eugene the Jeep is basically a magical mammal from the fourth dimension or some crazy, acid-trip shit like that.

Bluto (2008), Buena Vista Bank

Bluto is like that huge jerk at the bar, trying to hit on your girl. You realize (after a few beers) that he's actually your best bro friend—until you hate him again in the morning. Popeye used many a can of spinach to fight Bluto.

Sea Hag and Bernard (2010), Walmart

The devilish duo, the Sea Hag and pet vulture Bernard, are Popeye's true nemeses. Since Sea Hag is a woman and Popeye can't hit a lady, the characters got into some ridiculous altercations involving voodoo and tickling. Pop(eye) into Walmart after your visit with the hag to find a nemesis of your own.

Nephews (2016), Chester Grade School

This year's unveiling was pretty monumental. Peepeye, Poopeye, Pipeye, and Pupeye were Popeye's crazy little nephews, who looked more like sailor midgets than children. The nephews are a testament to the fact that E. C. Segar could get away with anything the fuck he wanted (e.g., naming characters "Poopeye").

THE WRIGHT STUFF

Arguably the greatest American architect of all time, Frank Lloyd Wright was a Midwestern boy with a dream to create structures that not only integrated the surrounding landscape into their design, but that spoke to humanity, and reflected a distinctive America architectural style. While everyone else was still building European-influenced structures, Wright went out on a limb and designed buildings in a different way; his all-American structures had strong geometric lines and a novel aesthetic.

PHILOSOPHY

Wright turned down a guaranteed career-booster education in Rome because he thought formal education lacked creativity. He wanted to change American architecture by designing so form followed function. Creating "organic" buildings to fit into the landscape, he was, according to Wright himself, "not an architect of structure but an architect of space" and many called him the cornerstone of modernism. Wright made things boxy but bright.

ARCHITECTURAL STYLES

Wright invented several styles of architecture that didn't exist before him, like the private homes he created in Chicago that captured the atmosphere around them.

He was the first to perfect "open plan" houses, which were small spaces with a lot of room, accented by tall windows that connected inside with outside and had a strong Japanese influence. Wright used the word *Usonian* to describe his style, which often consisted of flat roofs, concrete slabs, unique wall construction, and no basements or attics. He constructed homes with big communal areas; built-in tables, chairs, and fireplaces, and small private spaces encouraged people to mingle inside the house. Wright loved glass and was the first to install electric fixtures, floor lamps, and spherical hanging bulbs. He opted for open plans and "workspaces" (i.e., kitchens for women) because as servants were phased out of middle-class American life, women needed to see all the parts of the house while working in the kitchen or entertaining.

Notable structures in the Chicago area from his era of building houses for everyone in town include the Frederick C. Robie house, the Edward R. Hills house, and the Avery Coonley house. The concrete Unity Temple in Oak Park, Chicago, is nothing to look at from the outside. But inside, hard geometric lines sharply diverge from the design of traditional places of worship; that earned the temple its status as one of the top one hundred most significant buildings in the country.

WRIGHT GOES WEST

While early in his career he mostly worked in the Midwest, Wright's distinctive style spread to the coasts, and organically changed along the way. His textile block houses were built with a desire to wed machine-age techniques and organic architecture. He used large sheets of glass to blur the lines between inside and outside and created textile blocks from cement and decomposing granite. His idea was that these blocks were cheap, looked cool,

kept houses affordable, and made them look like they were growing on the site where they were built. In California, he also played around with Mayan architecture to create spectacular homes like the Ennis House in Los Feliz.

WRIGHT GOES EAST

While his West Coast structures were impressive, Wright's organic style fully blossomed when he created Fallingwater in Pennsylvania. The house, built for the Kaufmann family, wraps around a thirty-foot waterfall and floats in the space like a lavish rock formation. Similarly, the Graycliff estate referred to as the "Jewel on the Lake" sits high on a bluff over Lake Erie with views of the Canadian border and Buffalo, New York.

The grandaddy of Wright's eastern structures is NYC's Guggenheim Museum, built like a conch shell. Viewing art in this museum is a totally different experience than it is in boxier museum designs. Walking through its swirled middle ramp builds anticipation with the ascent, giving visitors a unique exhibit experience. Wright also designed the Price Tower in Bartlesville, Oklahoma, his only skyscraper, built to be reminiscent of "a tree that escaped the forest."

HOOSIER COUTURE

With Midwestern college girls uniformed in Uggs and black tights, game-changing fashion is probably the last thing you think of when it comes to the Midwest. But some of the most influential designers of 'Merica actually came from the heartland and were inspired by their humble hometowns to create glam garments.

BILL BLASS, INDIANA

No stranger to the high-fashion pages of *Vogue*, Bill Blass started his ascent as a fashion icon in Fort Wayne, Indiana. Bill began sewing and selling evening gowns to the big shots in New York, until he scrounged up enough coins to move to the city when he was just seventeen.

After working under (super-fancy man) Baron de Gunzburg, Bill took off on his own career ventures and began exploring the sporty-chic men's and women's wear he'd be known for over the next four decades. The designer's fame stretched far off the runway and onto the road in the form of auto interior design for Ford, where his nautical logos graced the Continental Mark in 1979's edition of the car. Blass went from selling Indiana-made dresses for $25 to a $700 million a year fashion empire. Among many other worthy awards, he was honored with a Lifetime Achievement Award by the Fashion Institute of Technology in 1999, three years before his death.

ROY HALSTON FROWICK, IOWA

Born in Des Moines, Iowa, Roy Halston Frowick eventually became just "Halston" and dressed the disco days divas to a tee. While he ruled the fashion world in many ways, his most recognizable design was Jackie O's pillbox hat.

Halston's idea of haute was frill-less fashion. He rid clothing of pointless bows, buttons, and clasps, and focused instead on flowy forms and functional shapes, using luxe fabrics like ultrasuede. He dated Venezuelan artist Victor Hugo for sixteen years and lived a life as lavish as his clothing, hitting Studio 54 with his famous model buds (called Halstonettes) regularly. Halston is a symbol of everything glam, with expensive fabrics dolled up with smart designs. He died in 1990 from a disease related to AIDS.

NORMAN NORELL, INDIANA

As a boy in Noblesville, Indiana, Norman always wanted to be an artist. He moved to New York and went to the Pratt Institute in Brooklyn to hone his craft. He designed costumes for Broadway, reflecting a penchant for the dramatic that was evident in his later ready-to-wear designs.

Norman was all about drama and elegance, and created mermaid sheath dresses, full-bottomed skirts lined with fur, and show-stopping embellishments and accessories. Norman loved Paris and imported his fabrics from Europe; he showed his line in collections, the way designers did across the pond. He brought back the natural waistline, and split skirts in the middle to controversially hint at pants in his 1960s shows. His fragrance, introduced in 1968 by Revlon, was the first successful designer perfume. Norman died in '72 at seventy-two in New York City, where he belonged.

STEPHEN SPROUSE, OHIO

The guy to thank (or blame) for incorporating Day-Glo graffiti and pop art into fashion, Stephen Sprouse came from more drab beginnings in Dayton, Ohio. He interned for fellow Midwesterners Bill Blass and Halston and broke out on his own to create more punk-driven designs in the '80s.

Sprouse sourced expensive fabrics and printed scribbled graffiti all over them in aggressive motifs. He outfitted greats like Debbie Harry, Duran Duran, and Billy Idol, and was arguably the man behind their recognizable party-punk aesthetic. Sprouse forced art and fashion to hold hands by printing Warhol's designs on his out-there fashions. He later hooked up with Louis Vuitton and took those rich bitch handbags, normally just brown and black, into an uncomfortable but fashionable color spectrum. While his designs defined an era, Sprouse never found the kind of fame Halston did, but, then again, he wasn't looking for it.

=== *Fun Fact* ===

Crawfordsville, Indiana, native Eleanor Lambert created the International Best Dressed List in 1940. Joan Rivers would have been just a yappy old broad without her.

FOOD

CHICAGO DOES SH*T DIFFERENTLY

Chicago isn't some warped world where everything gets flipped on its head (that's Austin), but they sure like to brag about how their different versions of things are best. From hot dogs to fine dining, here are a couple of things Chicagoans will defend to the death.

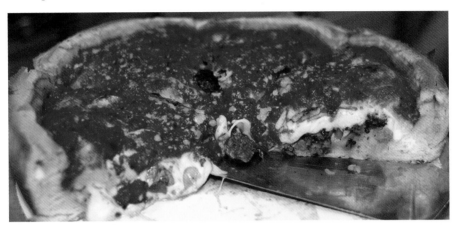

PIZZA

While the rest of the country is trying to figure out how to make translucently thin crust, Chicago says go deep, real deep. Chicago's iconic pizza style is more like a fatty meat pie than anything else. The crust is cakey and the fillings are generous. Chicagoans' idea of pizza is really upside down when it comes to deep dish, with the sauce hanging on the top, and the toppings, including cheese, blanketed underneath. You can hide a screwdriver in a Chicago-style pizza; what can you hide in yours, New York?

HOT DOGS

An all-American hot dog is a simple construction: white bun, dog, ketchup, mustard, and relish. In Chicago, that sort of dog just won't fly. First, the bun is dotted with poppy seeds, and then it gets "dragged through the garden" with the addition of many a pickled thing, like sweet relish, dill pickle, very specific sport peppers (pickled chilis from a jar),

=== *Fun Fact* ===

Chicago does do a thin-ish crust pizza, but it's more like cheesy bread, cut into bite-sized squares.

along with celery salt, diced onions, mustard, and sometimes tomato slices. This acidic dog is always all beef to keep it kosher, and if you even think of squirting on ketchup, prepare for death stares.

ITALIAN BEEF SANDWICH

On approach, this looks like a typical roast beef sandwich on an Italian roll, but look more closely; the thing is shimmering in liquid beef gold. It's an "au jus"–type deal, with giardiniera pickled bits mixed into thinly sliced, slow-roasted sirloin. This is one of those poor man sandwiches that came from Italian immigrants making the most of scraps. Chicago proudly exalts this native sandwich, sometimes stuffing a hot dog and cheese in between the beef to give it more bite.

OTP Tip: If you're a fan of just soggy bread (because who isn't?), Chicago offers "soakers" or "gravy bread," where an Italian roll is dipped in meat juice—nothing less, nothing more.

TAMALE BOAT

Other states have tamales and everyone makes their own version of chili, but only in Chicago do the two share a Styrofoam cup. The tamales in your chili boat aren't lovingly made by old Mexican lady hands; these are corn-roll tamales, extruded from a machine in perfect cylinders with

hamburger meat chillin' in the center. As with most things in Chicago, this can be made into a (hard-to-find) sandwich, this one called the "Mother-in-Law."

ALINEA

There are fancy restaurants and then there's Alinea, doing shit so differently that chef/owner Grant Achatz has been elevated to some sort of molecular gastronomy god, earning and keeping his three Michelin stars since 2011.

Alinea is known for deconstructing everything and putting it back together in unexpected ways. Where most tasting menus keep it in the single digits, Alinea serves eighteen to twenty-two dishes to round out the menus there. Dishes look like wacky, beautiful science experiments, because, well, they are. Dessert is made tabletop; not on a plate but on the table. Plus, the chef had mouth cancer in 2007 and kicked it in six months before it had any effect on his palate.

MINNESOTA VERSUS IOWA: STATE FAIR SHOWDOWN

Be it produce or locally crafted goods, the biggest pumpkin or the best-looking beaver, every state brings its proudest offerings to the fair every year, which is usually held close to the agricultural center of the state, near the capital if possible. But nobody is going to these things to see farmer Tom's hundred-pound zucchini. 'Mericans attend the fair to stuff their faces with absurd deep-fried things, preferably on a stick.

The entire country has been in a greasy battle for the grossest thing any-one can deep-fry, and both Minnesota and Iowa are known for their ungodly offerings. So who's clogging the most arteries?

IOWA	*versus*	MINNESOTA
Deep-fried butter stick–they've also sculpted a six-hundred-pound cow out of butter every year since 1911		Deep-fried spaghetti sticks– like mozzarella sticks, but made of fucking spaghetti
Cowboy cone–a waffle cone with pulled pork, coleslaw, beans, and BBQ sauce		Pig ears
Cheese curds		Cheese curds–they're neck and neck with Iowa on this one (or, should we say, double chin and double chin?)
Mac 'n' cheese with brisket and bacon bits sprinkled on top		Bread pudding
Double bacon corn dog, dipped in bacon bits and deep-fried twice		Gator sausage on a stick–or ostrich, if you prefer a different weird meat
Turkey leg		Turkey leg wrapped in bacon (take that, Iowa!)

TO BE FAIR . . .

Places like Texas and Florida also hold down their own appalling iterations of edible regret. Texas will fucking fry anything, including salsa, beer, bubblegum-flavored marshmallows, chicken fried bacon, pecan pie, Pop-Tarts, and all the candy bars!

Florida does Oreo burgers, deep-fried ice cream on top of a burger, and funnel-cake cheeseburgers. Basically, Florida can take any already-bad-for-you burger and make it so that it kills you right away. And you've gotta give it to Oklahoma for throwing a giant gummy bear in the deep fryer for a sight that'll parallel any Chucky nightmare you may have had.

Also, Arizona fries scorpions.

THE CHEESE CONTESTS OF WISCONSIN

If you take enough deep breaths in Wisconsin, the undisputed cheese capital of 'Merica, you'll eventually be able to extract a block of cheddar from your lungs. Here, the curd is always the word. Wisconsin's residents proudly call themselves "cheeseheads" and frequently go into fierce competition to separate the cheese royalty from the whey.

BUT FIRST, A LITTLE CHEESE-STORY

America's dairyland had humble beginnings. Expansive pastures allowed newly settled farmers to let their cows roam free and multiply, producing rich milk by the bucketful. In the mid-1800s, as a preservation tactic, people began making cheese from the abundance of milk. The industry exploded, new quality standards were established, and factories sprouted up, attracting European immigrants to contribute their cheesy stylings to the mix.

Old World cheeses were recreated in America, and new versions were developed and marketed to neighboring states. Wisconsin was the first state in 'Merica to create a milk-fat testing system and a cheese grading system. It is also the only state whose residents proudly wear foam cheese hats at every sporting event.

> ═══ *Fun Fact* ═══
>
> Elsewhere (Paris, California, New York), most people like pairing cheese with wine. In Wisconsin, beer washes down the dairy. Wisconsinites are also big on pairing their cheese with sausages. But who isn't?

U.S. CHAMPIONSHIP CHEESE CONTEST

This is the Olympics of cheese, and the winners are appropriately awarded solid-gold medals. This competition is as serious as getting your hand stuck in the cheese grater, and cheese heroes from all over the country gather to prove their milk-fat masses are the best.

It all began in 1980 when the Cheese-maker's Association called for the best of the best to be brought to the table for judgment in Madison. Today, over thirty thousand pounds of dairy, including butter and yogurt, are carefully evaluated in a number of categories. It doesn't matter if your cheese comes from a cow, a sheep, or a goat, nor whether it's Swiss, Gouda, or Mexican—everyone gets a shot at the gold. The proceeds from ticket sales ($35 a pop) all go to charity, and the cheese spectator samples all go toward maintaining your muffin top.

THE WISCONSIN STATE FAIR: CHEESE AND BUTTER CONTEST

Every state has a fair to celebrate its unique agricultural and industrial achievements.

No matter where you find yourself in 'Merica late in the summer, there will likely be a fair with games, rides, regional food, booze, and music.

The Wisconsin State Fair, held right outside of Milwaukee, is a little cheesier than other states. There's an official cheese and butter contest that draws dairy professionals from all around the state. Watching the judging is best done with deep-fried mac 'n' cheese on a stick, fried-cheese curds, and a Krispy Kreme cheeseburger (yeah, doughnut buns). The winning cheeses from the blue ribbon category are auctioned off, and you can walk away with a block of the best cheese in the country in one hand, and a pound of regret in the other.

> ═══ *Fun Fact* ═══
>
> In 2013, Wisconsin experimented with using cheese brine to salt down winter streets. We're not sure if it worked, but we're positive it must have smelled like a dream after a few days.

CHEESE DAYS:
COW MILKING CONTEST

You can't get competition-worthy cheese without feeling up some cows first. During Cheese Days in Monroe, an extravaganza of cheese, beer, and all things delicious, you can get some hands-on (teats) experience with cheesemaking. Dairy farmers bring their milkiest cows to the contest, and registered teams get to squeeze out the goods into buckets in front of amped-up cheeseheads. Cheese Days only happen on even years in mid-September, testing your cheese-loving patience to the extreme.

Wisconsin, a wonderland of cheese, is home to the Mars Cheese Castle (a fake castle with mountains of real cheese), countless cheese shops (the oldest of which is Baumgartner's), and one guy, Ed Zahn, who forgot about his cheddar blocks for twenty-eight years and then sold them for $6 per ounce to old-cheese lovers in 2012.

WHAT THE F*CK iS PROVEL?

Missouri's horrid idea of cheese, Provel is a processed white cheese that's made up of whateverthefuck. It's a mystery block that finds its way into many Missourian mouths in the form of pizza toppings. In fact, it was invented for the St. Louis–style pizza.

Can you cube it for wine and cheese parties? Fuck no. Provel is for (this weird interpretation of) pizza and nothing else. St. Louis is really the only place in the world that celebrates this mockery of dairy, and if you ever go at it raw, prepare to feel like you've been sucking on a candle that's spent its life shoved into an exhaust pipe. Those who grew up on it love it; those who were force-fed it, just to try it, hate it. Can you use it as a door stop? Sure thing.

MOTOWN

Remember when Yeezus was just Kim-less Kanye and everyone thought that he had the music formula all figured out? Well, Berry Gordy had him beat by a quick minute. Motown changed the soundscape of America forever, bringing R&B into the mainstream both carefully and with pizzazz.

HITMAKER

Berry Gordy Jr. was born in Detroit in 1929 and dropped out of high school because he wanted to be a boxer. He served in the Korean War, came back, made somewhat popular songs with his sister, and then reinvested his profits into building Motown and producing instead. Starting Motown with just a borrowed $800, Gordy set off to sign soon-to-be famous artists (like Smokey Robinson) to the label.

In the 60s, a time when America wasn't receptive to black artists, Gordy carefully controlled the images of his musicians in order to generate mass appeal. Some thought this was a cop-out; others sang his praises.

QUALITY CONTROL

Gordy held meetings where label execs would vote on what got released. He took black-ish music mainstream, and not just politically charged niche tunes or bluesy sounds from the oppressed South; this was mainstream pop that everone could enjoy. Was it a sellout? Maybe. But it brought black artists into the white-dominated music industry, allowing them to achieve levels of celebrity previously unavailable to them.

Gordy used to work on the Lincoln-Mercury production line and saw raw metal turn to shiny pieces, then eventually into cars. This is the process he wanted to apply

to musicians. Gordy put the Temptations, Smokey Robinson, Diana Ross, the Jackson Five, and many others through his music production line and they all came out shining stars on the other side. Gordy didn't quite promote revolution music, but that doesn't make what he did any less revolutionary. The biggest black-owned business of the time, Hitsville U.S.A. was a music-making factory, and pumped out an incredible 180 no. 1 songs.

> ===== *Fun Fact* =====
> Berry Gordy is Jimmy Carter's cousin.

WAS IT TOO VANILLA?

During the '60s, there was a lot of politically charged music that Gordy stayed away from. The atmosphere was tense, but Gordy chose to focus on positive themes like love, producing game-changing songs like "My Girl" by the Temptations, "Baby Love" by the Supremes, and (our very favorite), "Brick House" by the Commodores.

Revolutionary music was known for its double entendres, but Gordy mostly steered clear of that, too, with the exception of "Dancing in the Street," first recorded by Martha and the Vandellas. That was supposed to be a fun summer song, but was interpreted as a call to riot in the streets. Gordy's goal was to blur the racial divide by producing good music. Period.

> ===== *Fun Fact* =====
> At the end of 1963, *Billboard* magazine discontinued its R&B chart in favor of a single pop-music Top 100, having determined that white and black record-buying trends could no longer be meaningfully distinguished. At the beginning of 1965, the year Malcolm X was assassinated, *Billboard* reinstated the R&B chart, because white and black tastes were diverging again.

BROKEN RECORD

In the '70s, the label moved to Los Angeles, and nothing has been the same since. Motown got some of its soul from Detroit, and LA lacked the gusto. Gordy sold his rights, some of the big names either left or died, and the fortunes of the legendary label declined sharply. Even though it no longer has the same status it once had, Motown will always be relevant and revered for its unparalleled influence on the music industry.

OHIO'S FAMOUS MUSICIANS

You'd expect weird experimental garage grunge to come out of Ohio (and some does), but not huge names. In one of the weirdest phenomena in 'Merica, Ohio somehow pumps out a shit ton of famous musicians. Perhaps it's the boredom that makes people in the Buckeye State pick up a guitar and start belting out memorable tunes. Whatever it is, Ohio is fertile ground for sound. Here are a few of the very different musical masters to come from the Buckeye State.

BLACK KEYS

Famously hailing from Akron, the Black Keys is a two-man band—the grungy denim-and-flannel-loving Dan Auerbach and Patrick Carney—that made it so big that their 2012 show sold out Madison Square Garden in minutes. Whether you love or hate the Keys' pop-grunge vibe, the duo has seven hit albums, and while they might sound like a White Stripes knockoff, their impact on music is undeniable, even if Michael Bublé's Christmas album kept *El Camino* from hitting number one on the charts.

BOBBY WOMACK

One of the coolest dudes ever, Bobby Womack had the kind of swagger we can't imagine he learned in Cleveland. Bobby started his music career in a cutesy sibling band, fronted by his brother, called Curtis Womack and the Womack Brothers. After the Stones stole their song "It's All Over Now," Bobby got to work carving out a spot in history for himself.

Following seven decades on the music scene with hits like "If You Think You're Lonely Now," Womack was inducted into the Rock and Roll Hall of Fame in 2009. *Jackie Brown* (one of our favorite movies) would never be the same without Womack's "Across 110th Street" on the soundtrack.

=== *Fun Fact* ===

The Isley Brothers (from Cincinnati) is the only musical group in history to be in the Billboard Top 40 in six separate decades.

MARILYN MANSON

Marilyn Manson creeped everyone out beyond belief, and rumors of him being the kid from *Mr. Belvedere* (or perhaps Mr. Belvedere himself) were only recently put to bed. His real name is Brian Hugh Warner, which just sounds like your mild-mannered roommate and not the crazy creep man we all know and (sort of) love. *Antichrist Superstar*, Marilyn Manson's second studio album, made him an overnight success, and *The Beautiful People* still sends chills down our spines. His cover of the Eurythmics' "Sweet Dreams" is so fucking twisted it's hard to get through the whole tune without making sure all the doors are locked. Born in Canton, the black-outfitted, mutilation-loving Marilyn likely emerged from the loins of the devil himself.

DAVE GROHL

Dave drummed his way into our hearts via Nirvana and the Foo Fighters. The nicest dude (and dad) ever, Dave was born in Warren and hasn't skipped a beat since the '90s. Dave isn't just one of the best (two-armed) drummers in history—the guy is also hilarious. The Foo Fighters didn't fuck around when it came to videos (many of which Grohl directed), and each one of them had some quirky theme. We now know that Grohl plays a great '70s soap opera doctor ("The Long Road to Ruin"), can pretend-pilot a plane of crazy people—most of which were played by him ("Learn to Fly")—and, of course, swings a mean huge-hand backhand ("Everlong"). There's nothing that Grohl can't do, except for maybe sit still for an hour.

> === *Fun Fact* ===
>
> Dave Grohl drinks so much coffee that he was once hospitalized after an overdose. Fresh pots!

THE ROCK AND ROLL HALL OF FAME

The only reason to ever go to Cleveland, the Rock and Roll Hall of Fame is a collection of music legends from all genres. Sitting pretty on Rock and Roll Boulevard on the shores of Lake Erie, this music shrine has been around only since 1995. Getting inducted isn't easy, nor is the process all that fair. But as far as Halls of Fame go, this one's the big kahuna.

WHY CLEVELAND?

While many cities were considered (like Memphis or NYC, which would make a lot more sense), Cleveland won out by its pledge of $65 million from the city to construct it. The money may have swung the votes in Cleveland's favor, but the city wasn't completely devoid of claims to fame.

Alan Freed, a DJ at Cleveland radio station WJW, is credited with coining the term *rock and roll* back in 1951. He used it to describe R&B records he'd throw on the waves. The Moondog Coronation Ball—a concert held at the Cleveland Arena in 1952 that was called off after the first act due to overcapacity issues—is widely accepted as the first rock and roll concert in America. WMMS was a local radio station that broke acts like David Bowie, and when music fans were polled, Cleveland somehow won over Memphis as the desired location for the Hall of Fame.

TICKET TO FAME

Founded by various music moguls and the publisher of *Rolling Stone*, the Hall of Fame opened its doors in 1995 as a collection of rock's major players. A grand opening concert that featured Iggy Pop, James Brown, Bruce Springsteen, and Johnny Cash, among an impressive collection of others, was thrown together to promote the newly opened Hall, and sent the message that getting your name past its doors would be a feat.

So how do you go about getting inducted? Well, it's tricky and kind of shady. Officially, an artist must have released a record twenty-five years prior to induction, have an influential body of work, and demonstrate "unquestionable musical excellence." Unofficially, you've gotta shake some hands.

MEET YOUR MUSIC

In addition to an extensive library of music, a full history of rock 'n' roll, and exhibits, the Hall holds all kinds of public events that get you within arm's reach of your favorite musicians in a setting that's not a sweaty, screaming concert. The Hall of Fame Series began in 1996 and puts various musicians in the spotlight, not to sing but to talk. These interviews give fans a chance to get up close and real personal with people who normally just sweat on them. We would have killed to chat with Darryl "D.M.C." Matthews McDaniels back in 2009. The Hall frequently holds events, like the annual American Music Masters Series, where fans get friendly with inductees and are treated to weeklong events and an all-star concert finale at the Cleveland Theater.

===== *Fun Fact* =====

Despite their fame, the Monkees are excluded from the Hall for reasons unknown.

LAKE PARTY PEOPLE

When the ocean is a flight away, you make do with what you've got, and while partying on a lake may not be a proper beach, it's not the pits, either. In the end, water is water, and wearing next to nothing near it will always result in wet, wild, and wacky fun. The Lake of the Ozarks in Missouri really captures the spirit of making the most out of a lake come summer.

THE LAY OF THE LAKE

This isn't some dinky watering hole. The Lake of the Ozarks is a reservoir pumped with water from the Osage and other rivers. A grand 55,000 acres, the lake boasts 1,150 miles of shoreline that serpentines around the state, creating nooks and crannies perfect for partying. When a lake is nicknamed the "Magic Dragon," you know that nothing but good times are ahead.

PARTY COVE

Party Cove is, well, exactly that. Formally called "Hollow Cove," this inlet of the lake not only attracts over three thousand boats for the Fourth of July weekend, but is a giant floating party whenever the sun is shining. Follow the great boat migration—a giant water world of Jet Skis, putt putts, and rich-man catamarans—to an aquatic party that's been drunkenly blasting through the wakes for decades.

Watch out for the "gauntlet," where two parallel rows of boats subject new seafarers to water balloons, serious Super Soaker action, and a steady stream of insults. With ridiculous yachts and lax laws on toplessness, it's a raunchy water party where anything goes.

AQUAPALOOZA

While Party Cove is an ongoing celebration of beer, rum, and the waters that make consuming them a dangerous pit of death, AquaPalooza is an organized one-day event with sponsors, radio stations, cover band concerts, and some of the same boat-y revelry, but with more children. A traveling aqua party, it goes down mid-July at the Dog Days Bar & Grill in Osage Beach, and tours the lakes of the country for the rest of summer.

MORE-SSOURI

Once you get all the water out of your ears and the booze out of your system, check out the other wonders Missouri has to offer. Watch the Angel showers gush from the rock cave ceiling at Ozark Caverns, explore the Bonne Terre Mines (a human-made miracle cavern that'll take your breath away), get up high at Taum Sauk Mountain (the highest point in Missouri), and climb around the Johnson's Shut-In State Park (a naturally formed water park). Then slip into the peaceful campgrounds of Table Rock Mountain to relax for a while.

THE ART OF THE SUPER BOWL PARTY

Every year, the entire country rages with Super Bowl Sunday parties and a good chunk of the population calls in sick the following Monday. Part of Midwestern identity is an undying love for the Super Bowl. And it's not just pro football; it's the festivities that surround this near-national holiday. Pounding beers is part of the deal, but there are several nuances that take a Midwestern football party from good to super.

are just known for never making it into the Bowl (looking at you, Cleveland Browns!). Pick a team and stick with it. Buy the apparel and learn the secret handshake. Nobody in the Midwest likes a half-assed fan.

KNOW YOUR SNACKS

The rest of the country has a standard game-day menu that consists of wings, chips and dips, burgers, loaded potato skins, and beer. In the Midwest, it's all that stuff, plus mayo, bologna, and Applebee's- and TGI Friday's-inspired sensations. If "cooking" isn't in the playbooks, expect a heaping load of taco-esque finger food from Taco

KNOW YOUR TEAMS

There are two conferences: the AFC and the NFC. Midwestern teams are known as well for whining (go Green Bay Packers) as for losing (boo Minnesota Vikings). Others

Bell, meat on meat with meat from Arby's, or convenience-store hot dogs, with plenty of mayo squirt packets on the side. We're kidding, sort of.

HALFTIME

If you don't know shit about football but want to impress Midwestern party hosts, here are a few talking points about notable halftime shows.

Super Bowl I (1967)

Two guys from Bell Aerosystems strapped on jetpacks and flew around the stadium to the "oohs" and "ahhs" of the space-age crowd.

Super Bowl XXVII (1993)

Michael Jackson, pre-molestation accusation, was surrounded by 3,500 local children to sing "Heal the World."

=== *Fun Fact* ===

One of OTP's cofounders sang her heart out in a yellow sweatshirt onstage with the King of Pop that year.

Super Bowl XXXVIII (2004)

Justin Timberlake and Janet Jackson were performing a duet when a "wardrobe malfunction" sparked panic in the stadium. Justin pulled at Janet's bra-top contraption and her boob flopped out. This event will forever be referred to as "Nipplegate."

COMMERCIALS

Football fans outnumber baseball fans by about thirty million and, come game day, big companies know that people's eyes are fixated on the big game. For this reason, the most expensive ads run during the Super Bowl. Advertisers aim to gain new customers with humor, glitz, drama, and a fair amount of food porn (or almost actual porn). Should you find yourself glued to the tube in the Midwest, know that everyone is looking for that big Budweiser or Coors commercial. Once it comes on, get your beers ready, 'cause it's pounding time.

When the season ends, Midwesterners feel empty and, as such, get way too involved in fantasy football or any other way to keep the good times rolling while the pro players recover.

METRO MAKEOUT SPOTS

Big city lights aren't exactly what comes to mind when we talk about the Midwest, and while America's heartland is indeed covered in cornfields in some parts, thriving singles scenes are scattered around in the big cities of the country's midsection. From sexy dives to posh parties, the Midwestern metro areas offer limitless makeout opportunities. Here are five places your chances of driving a tractor are lower and your chances of plowing a Midwesterner are higher.

STUDIO L'AMOUR, CHICAGO, ILLINOIS

This one's for the sapiosexuals out there. A school where you can learn the art of seduction, there's burlesque and all kinds of sexiness going on. The "dojo for your mojo" holds an event called "Naked Girls Reading," which is made up of one part naked girls, and another part linguistic stimulation. At this BYOB event, ain't nobody leavin' without at least a word boner.

OHIO RIVER, CINCINNATI, OHIO

The Over-the-Rhine neighborhood has plenty of great bars to pick up a makeout partner (like elixir-hawking Sundry & Vice and Neons Unplugged, with oversized Jenga outside and heavy PDA all over). But to really seal the lip-locking deal, drag your new saliva friend across the Purple People Bridge to the shore of the Ohio River and settle down to gaze at the stadium while little boats float by. If it's game day and

Cincy wins, your makeout session will be accompanied by fireworks ignited from a rock's throw away.

THE SLIPPERY NOODLE INN, INDIANAPOLIS, INDIANA

Indianapolis didn't get the twelfth highest rank in STDs just sitting around on its Midwestern bum. People hook up here, and the oldest, most aptly named dive bar where folks get down and dirty is the Slippery Noodle Inn. The dive bar wiggled onto the scene in 1850, has old gangster bullets lodged in the walls, is rumored to be haunted, and serves $3 Crown shots to guarantee you're good and sloppy in no time. Make sure to bring a rubber for your slippery noodle, just in case.

TRINITY THREE IRISH PUBS, MILWAUKEE, WISCONSIN

If one Irish pub has the power to drop panties, imagine what three interconnected ones can do. Trinity Three Irish

Pubs are full of dark nooks and crannies, like an Irish muffin if the English would let them make one. This Irish pub supercenter, with a bar, dining room, and music area, makes sure you get tongue-glued to some unsuspecting stranger by serving up $3 car bombs. There's live music on the weekends and beer pong every Thursday.

MOOLAH THEATER & LOUNGE, ST. LOUIS, MISSOURI

In St. Louis, nudity and liquor licenses don't mix. Take your grope sessions to the movies, as you did in high school, but better. Your exposed skin will be gleefully stuck to the theater's leather seats, your mouth wrapped around movie-themed drinks, your eyes occupied with whatever's playing on the big screen, and your hands busy trying to figure out the fleshy bits in the dark. The theater is housed in an old Shriners temple and *Moolah* is Arabic for "Title for one learned in teaching dignity for the law of the Qur'an or religion." So whatever you do in here, do it with dignity.

HOW TO WOO A MIDWESTERNER

If you're going to be hanging out in the middle of nowhere, having someone to hold your hand, or at least steer the tractor, is lovely. Here's how to tap into the romantic side of the hardworking heartland.

WALMART DATE NIGHT

Walmart is filled with endless possibilities. Aside from aisles of Cheez Whiz and Pixy Stix, the best people-watching opportunities in the world are right here, which makes for hours of date-night entertainment.

PAY STUBS

Bring your pay stubs everywhere! There's nothing sexier here than a full-time job with benefits.

ROMANTIC DINNER

Put away your dress shirts and credit cards; in the Midwest, romantic meals consist of cheese, or something dipped in cheese and/or ranch dressing. A tater tot casserole paired with the finest Budweiser will do. If you're really looking to impress, Olive Garden (unlimited salad and breadsticks fo' life!), Cheesecake Factory, or anywhere with a buffet (Golden Corral) is sure to woo.

SOLVE THE SH*T OUT OF A CORN MAZE

In the land of corn, knowing your way around a maize maze is a big deal. Stick to making a bunch of right turns and you'll likely find the exit. Getting lost and subsequently feeling terrified will tap into your sensitive, emotional side. Win-win even if you lose-lose.

BE SERIOUSLY NICE

. . . to the point where it's suspicious. If you just can't find it in your soul to be kind, go on and on about how you love David Letterman (from Indiana), Bill Murray (from Illinois), and Jim Gaffigan (also from Illinois).

ALASKA

CANADA →
→

Fairbanks

BERING
SEA

Matanuska
Glacier

Anchorage

GULF OF
ALASKA

↑ CANADA ↑

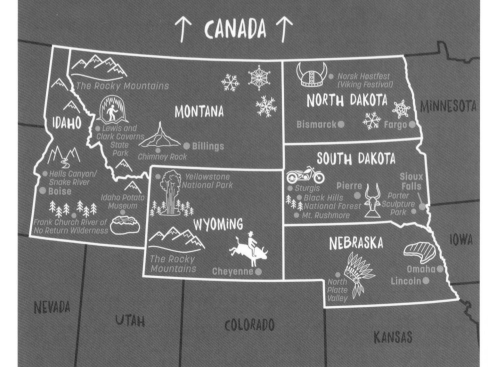

The Rocky Mountains

MONTANA

IDAHO

Lewis and
Clark Caverns
State
Park

Chimney Rock

Billings

Norsk Høstfest
(Viking Festival)

NORTH DAKOTA

MINNESOTA

Bismarck

Fargo

Hells Canyon/
Snake River

Boise

Idaho Potato
Museum

Frank Church River of
No Return Wilderness

Yellowstone
National Park

WYOMING

The Rocky
Mountains

Cheyenne

SOUTH DAKOTA

Sturgis
Black Hills
National Forest
Mt. Rushmore

Pierre

Sioux
Falls

Porter
Sculpture
Park

NEBRASKA

North
Platte
Valley

Omaha

Lincoln

IOWA

NEVADA

UTAH

COLORADO

KANSAS

NEBRASKA
AND THE LIKE

While many think this is no-man's territory, only necessary as a land connection between East and West, you'd be missing out on a whole lotta buffalo if you didn't drop into the Northern Plains. Sure, North Dakota is flat as fuck, but the exploding geysers of Yellowstone, the curious faces of Mount Rushmore, and the glorious attractions of Montana (that's right, Montana!) make it more entertaining. What do we mean by "the Like"? It's our clever way to add Alaska to the mix. If you come to this part of the country for one thing, let it be the Testy Festy, Montana's annual showcase of testosterone, where the main event is gobbling gonads.

INTO THE WILD

With fewer big-city distractions, the best thing to do in this vast region is get outdoors. If this is the land where the buffalo roam, we think doing a little wandering in the wilderness ourselves is in order. From steep mountain ranges to fast-moving rivers, these are five spots that deliver the greatest outdoor adventures in the Northern Plains. Word to the wise: Don't eat the berries to avoid dying ironically of starvation.

HELLS CANYON, IDAHO BORDER

Spanning the border separating Idaho from Oregon, this 652,488 acres of Earth is the deepest river gorge in 'Merica. You can explore the giant gash by car, on foot, or by boat. The great Snake River, which originates in Yellowstone, winds through this wilderness, where you'll find swiftly changing terrain, incredible rock formations, and rare vegetation. This devilish place is the result of tectonic plate movement a cool 150 million years ago. While Satan himself unleashed his fiery fury on Idaho's wilderness, burning much of it in 2006, the Seven

Devils Mountains still stand as a challenge for anyone brave enough to endure hell (i.e., elevations above nine thousand feet at He Devil Peak) for bragging rights.

WHITE BUTTE, NORTH DAKOTA

When North Dakotans aren't chiseling cows out of fiberglass (visit Sue in New Salem), they're ripping through some rugged terrain at White Butte, the state's highest point at an elevation of 3,507 feet. It's a cold and windy ascent to the top—with many a mosquito in the air—but it offers picturesque views of the state's otherwise

flatlands. If you prefer darkness to light, Black Butte is the second highest point in the state at an elevation of 3,465 feet. Visit in the spring or fall when the rattlesnakes that slither around the Butte are sleeping.

> === *Fun Fact* ===
>
> You don't have to go to Egypt to see a human-made pyramid. Nekoma, North Dakota, is home to a super-weird pyramid made in the 1960s to track Soviet missiles.

RIVER OF NO RETURN, IDAHO

In the middle of the Frank Church Wilderness (named after a U.S. senator in 1984), the banks of this river are for animal lovers. This place is packed with mountain lions, gray wolves, black bears, red foxes, elk, mountain goats, a variety of deer, and good ol' beavers. Why aren't you returning from this river? Well, back in the day, boats were able to navigate down the river but not back up, due to fast-moving water and rapids. These days, you'll probably never come back from the Main Salmon River (its updated name), because of all the wildlife you'll befriend. Watch out for critters with rabies.

NORTH PLATTE VALLEY, NEBRASKA

You're going to look at a whole lot of rocks; impressive ones, but still rocks. Courthouse and Jail Rocks stick out 400 feet from the valley, piercing the sky with their majestic formations. Many early pioneers on the Oregon Trail documented these rocks in their diaries and found it hard to believe they weren't human-made, because they look as if the wind picked up a chisel. Twelve miles down the trail, Chimney Rock is another impressive natural feat. While lesser rocks have eroded into dust, Chimney Rock's sharp spire, at 325 feet, is as tall as it has always been.

MATANUSKA GLACIER, ALASKA

If you can actually make it to Alaska, unlike the guy from *Into the Wild*, the Matanuska Glacier is a sight for wilderness-obsessed eyes. The largest glacier in Alaska that can be reached by vehicle, this twenty-six-mile-long solid body of ice has not changed in ten thousand years. The glacier is the town's weather fairy, pushing warm air upward to the mountain peaks with its cold body, making for sunny skies. Slow crying to Eddie Vedder when you get there is optional but recommended.

MONTANA IS ACTUALLY KIND OF GREAT

With 'Merica's iconic places, like New York City and the bright lights of Hollywood, Montana doesn't quite make it to U.S. destination bucket lists. We're here to tell you to pack your rucksack full of bison jerky and hightail it to Montana, a state with surprisingly cool things to see and do. Plus, there's no sales tax, so you can go wild on frivolous purchases.

GRASSHOPPER GLACIER

Glaciers are pretty cool as is. But add an ancient frozen grasshopper from a snowstorm long, long ago to the ice mass and you've got yourself an archaeological good time. The Grasshopper Glacier, located in the Beartooth Mountains, contains more than just solid water. Scientists discovered millions of extinct grasshoppers (later identified as locusts), stuck inside the massive glacier from over two hundred years ago. Climate change has exposed many of these insects to the elements, and they can be dug up with a few good finger scrapes. The glacier is melting, so get there before these grasshoppers join their brethren in the sewer systems of 'Merica.

LEWIS AND CLARK CAVERNS

Did the famous expedition lead to the discovery of these here caverns? It absolutely did not. This misleading name was all Teddy Roosevelt's fault when he decided to name it after the famous pioneers for the sole reason that there was no other national monument named after them at the time. Nonetheless, these caverns are

pretty cool. While during the summer days the rock formations get a lot of kiddy eyeballs on them, the candlelit winter night viewings (in December) are an amazing sight to behold.

OTP Tip: If you're really itching for some historical artifacts, you can see Clark's autograph on Pompeys Pillar nearby.

SKIJORING

The fuck is that, you ask? Well, you grab yourself a rope and some skis, get your friend to straddle a horse, and lasso onto him as he drags you through the snow. It's basically like a Montana cold-weather

rodeo, or waterskiing where the water is snow and the boat is a horse. A relative of the Scandinavian variation involving dogs, the skijoring World Championships are held in Whitefish on the last weekend in January.

OH YEAH, YELLOWSTONE!

While most of the park lies in adjacent Wyoming, the hottest geyser of Yellowstone bursts out in Montana. The Norris Geyser Basin is full of super-hot geothermal activity, including Steamboat Geyser, the tallest water spewer in the world. Come here for a natural steam facial and a full frontal water assault.

OTP Tip: If you're a fly fisher, get out to Paradise Valley, 'Merica's premier destination for throwing sharp objects at sea life.

You say you want casinos? While a certain degree of gambling is legal in the state, you won't find Vegas-type glitz here. What you will find are machines inside bars and resorts that'll give you that zombie glow if you want it.

THE COLORS OF YELLOWSTONE

Wyoming is the last state alphabetically in that song you learned in elementary school, but it's the first when it comes to adventure, largely due to Yellowstone Park. The expansive wilderness of the world's first official national park (est. 1872)—it kisses parts of Minnesota and Idaho, too—is a giant bubbling beautiful mess, where shooting geysers, hot springs, and running bison are sights to be seen. From the yellow sandstones running along the river that gave the park its name, to the rainbow-colored Tower Falls, you can spend a month uncovering the spectrum of the 2.2 million acres of Yellowstone. Here are five picks to get you started.

River, and misty steam floats around to add drama. If you're a fan of falls, Yellowstone has a handful that'll make you swoon. Tower Falls is a majestic sight, the lower Yellowstone Falls is a giant 308-footer that looks like a painting, and upper Yellowstone Falls is its little brother, a 109-foot guzzler.

OLD FAITHFUL

If you want to see hot water shooting from the ground, 180.5 feet in the air, Old Faithful will never disappoint. While he's not the biggest in the park, he's got the motion of the ocean thing down pat. How faithful is this old geyser? He erupts about every ninety minutes, and doesn't even ask for a sandwich afterward. If you want to cheat on Old Faithful, hit up the rest of the geyser basins, including the semifaithful Lone Star Geyser (which erupts every three hours or so), Steamboat (the world's tallest geyser), and the super-hot Black Growler Steam Vent (where clouds of steam hiss out at up to 280 degrees).

TOWER FALLS

This plunging waterfall rushes down 132 feet from towering rock pinnacles, and if you stand here long enough, seeing a rainbow is almost guaranteed. The falls hit a rocky gorge that meets the Yellowstone

=== *Fun Fact* ===

The Yellowstone River is the longest undammed river in the United States.

BOILING RIVER

Start at the Mammoth Hot Springs, a collection of limestone-lined white springs fueled by the geyser basins nearby. You can't swim in these calcified springs, but just a skip south, the Boiling River is a naturally occurring, hot-water swimming spot that attracts humans and animals alike. The water of Boiling River is the runoff from hydrothermal features and will make your skin shimmer. Yellowstone will provide the Jacuzzi, you bring the champagne.

GRAND CANYON OF YELLOWSTONE

Not as grand as the grand Grand Canyon, but still pretty fucking grand. This gaping canyon is twenty-four miles long, with patches of bright red oxidized rock and a rolling river capped by waterfalls on either end. As far as geologic features go, this one's just a wee baby at about fourteen thousand years old, created by erosion with the help of the Yellowstone River.

OTP Tip: The valleys, particularly Hayden and Lamar, are where the buffalo (and sometimes wolf packs) actually roam.

GRAND PRISMATIC SPRING

Remember how, if you licked a jawbreaker enough to get to its middle, the interior would reveal rings of colors that formed a rainbow? This place looks exactly like that, minus all the sugar, plus a bunch of naturally occurring hot water.

The largest hot spring in the States, this alien landscape gets its colors from turquoise-colored bacteria floating around near the water's surface, which is surrounded by fiery red and orange algae on its rim. The spring was discovered two hundred years ago and has been bewildering visitors ever since.

OTP Tip: The Yellowstone Caldera (aka Super Volcano) erupts every sixteen hundred years, and its last blast blew chunks as far as Mexico.

ART *and* DESIGN

MOUNT RUSHMORE

Wait, wait, before you get too excited, this thing is pretty disappointing, but these sculptures of dead presidents on the side of a mountain are iconic, and you must pay them a visit, lest you want to be seen as unpatriotic. The shrine of democracy may be a little lacking in size, but these mountain mugs bring over three million annual visitors to look up their stone noses. So what's the big deal?

WHY CARVE A CLIFF?

In the '20s, tourism to the desolate hills of South Dakota was low. In an effort to pique people's interest, a local historian had a grand idea: Carve famous people into their abundant supply of rock and call it something cool, like the "Shrine of Democracy."

Gutzon Borglum was hired for the task, and drew up some ideas in 1925. Borglum's vision included the presidents' busts, torso and all, but funds were cut short. It took four hundred workers to remove 45,000 tons of rock to make these sixty-foot faces possible. Dynamite and pneumatic hammers were used to blast the shit out of the rock, while chisels and drills were used for the sculpted artistic parts. The mountain sculpture was completed in 1941, the same year its designer kicked the bucket.

===== *Fun Fact* =====

Who the fuck is Rushmore? He was a New Yorker who traveled to the hills to figure out if he could mine them for profit. He made friends with locals who named the mountain after him.

STONE-COLD OLD DUDES

So what was so special about these guys that their faces were chosen to be set in

Gutzon Borglum's Model of Mt. Rushmore Memorial Washington, Jefferson, Roosevelt & Lincoln

stone for all eternity? Well, aside from the fact that at the time they drew the biggest crowds, each former president had a few lovable quirks that kept the spectators interested.

George Washington

The first to rule this fine nation under God, Washington was essentially the first start-up CEO of our time. He had to figure out how the hell to run a completely wacked-out, disjointed country while keeping his cool and wearing a powdery wig.

Thomas Jefferson

The third president of 'Merica penned the Declaration of Independence, loved his literature, and bullshitted about economics like it was his job (which it sort of was). He also owned slaves, but took them to Paris with him.

Theodore Roosevelt

Affectionately called "Teddy," the cuddly twenty-sixth president was the youngest to take office at forty-two years old. Teddy's motto was to "speak softly and carry a big stick," which 'Merica still takes to heart. In addition to his stone face on the mount, his name forever lives on in

stuffed form, as the teddy bear got its name from President Roosevelt's affection toward woodland creatures.

Abraham Lincoln

The grandaddy of freedom, Abe was a stand-up dude. The beard behind the Emancipation Proclamation, he was the only president to hold a patent (for flotation systems alongside boats for navigation in shallow waters). Lincoln could have invented Uber; it was just a different time.

SAW IT. NOW WHAT?

Don't feel as if you got your fill of mountain face carvings? Check out the unfinished Crazy Horse Memorial. If you need more mountain, head south to Georgia to see the sculpture of famous Confederate General Robert E. Lee on Georgia's Stone Mountain, done by the same designer as Rushmore.

Like your presidents sans mountain? Rapid City, South Dakota, is the City of Presidents, where a life-sized sculpture of a president creeps on every corner, with forty-three presidents represented. Snuggle up to Bill Clinton, take a selfie with Dwight D. Eisenhower, and give Jimmy Carter's outstretched hand a stinging high-five.

ART DAKOTA: PORTER SCULPTURE PARK

South Dakota is known for, well, all kinds of nothing. Mount Rushmore maybe—but mostly nothing. Porter Sculpture Park defies all boring odds. When you're from a state where the most famous person from your state is your local farmer, being Wayne Porter is pretty nice. His cobbled-together metal sculptures make you wonder how many other talented weirdos are lurking in the flat planes of the Mount Rushmore state.

THE MAN

In Montrose, South Dakota, the works of Wayne Porter stick out like a soaring thumb. He builds giant works in small pieces, sometimes spending years on them and ultimately not knowing if they'll work when he puts them together. Luckily, living in South Dakota affords him all the time in the world.

His father was a blacksmith and Wayne started cobbling together parts when he was in high school. A vegetarian, Wayne builds towering tributes to animals and human forms alike, with trippy, psychedelic sculptures that boggle the imagination. He describes himself as "naturally twisted," a perfect backstory to this display of weirdness.

OTP Tip: Visit the park in the summer, from Memorial Day to Labor Day, when Wayne hangs out in a shack that he built near his sculptures and gives tours soundtracked by his charming chatter.

THE ART

The open-range park consists of more than fifty sculptures Wayne hand-built using industrial equipment (like a cement mixer) and welded-together scraps. The largest sculpture, a horned bull head, is sixty feet tall, weighs twenty-five tons, and is about the same size as a head on Rushmore.

In addition to the bull head, the park contains several metallic dragons; a screaming head with a hand protruding from the top; a huge, yellow hand with a perched butterfly on its pointer finger; and a collection of goldfish, propped up with various metal poles and loops to make them look like they're swimming around the prairie.

THE MESSAGE

Every piece has a story. "Hammer" was built to commemorate the five hammers Wayne broke building his roadside shack. Handwritten signs to describe what in the fuck Wayne was thinking when he built them poke through the dirt near some of the wacky works of art. Meandering through the park will make you realize that Wayne's not as crazy as he seems; many of his sculptures somehow tell the story of the human condition.

The perched buzzards, holding knives, forks, anvils, and mallets, are symbols of power-hungry politicians, while the battling boars evoke the violence condoned by our society. Some themes allude to happiness, and many of Wayne's works are inspired by Greek, Roman, and Egyptian art and design. The crevices of the weathered sculptures are occasionally inhabited by field mice, birds, and other critters, adding to the sculptures' connection to the land around them.

WEARING WALRUS

The Inuit battle weather conditions city folk can't even fathom: temps at fifty-five degrees below zero, winds coming at your face like a freight train, and enough snow to keep a bulldozer busy for months. Alaskan winters are no joke, and wearing a carcass is sometimes the only way to get through it.

The Inuit aren't focused on being chic; it's all about badassery and survival. They use anything and everything to create fashions that keep them alive. Can you wear that hide? The Inuit say, "Hell yes!"

WALRUS GUT PARKA

A *sanightaaq* is a ceremonial parka made from the dried guts of bearded seals or walruses, worn to ask the gods for a good hunt. And around these parts, you don't just wear your parka plain; it gets decked out in crushed-up beaks of Alaskan birds, trimmed with baby walrus fur, and strips of sealskin around the hood.

CARIBOU COATS

Sure, a bear or fox skin will keep you cozy, but caribou is special. The individual hairs of the 'bou are hollow so that they trap heat both between and inside the hair. As such, caribou pelts are ideal for fluffy coats, sometimes worn in pairs with one coat that is insulated with fur inside and an overcoat with fur on the outside. What happens when you get a back itch? You mind-over-matter that shit.

SEALSKIN BOOTS

Called *payaaqek*, these fancy, knee-high boots are made by bleaching the skins of seals out in the frigid air of winter. While they're made to be functional, using sealskin as a water-resistant material, they are also crafted with a bit of fashion and tradition in mind. A thin red line, called *atngaghun*, runs down the middle of the boots and is said to symbolize the traditional face tats of Inuit women.

WOLF HATS

Trapper hats are for mainland newbs. In Alaska, you wear the whole damn wolf on your head. Wolf and wolverine fur is known for its ability to shed snow faster than any other fur, and the Inuit tap into that power. Here, the wolf is regarded as a sacred animal, and, traditionally, when one is killed, a man will walk around the house four times and not have sex with his wife for four days.

CARCASS ACCESSORIES

Necklace and bracelet cords are made primarily from guts, with orca guts being a popular material. Decorative pieces are carved out of ivory, bones, and antlers. Caribou teeth and beads are used as decoration on headbands made of skins. While we pierce our faces for looks, labrets are symbolic piercings where puberty-aged boys get their lower lip sliced and plugged with bones or stones.

> ### *Fun Fact*
>
> Lady Inuit must be expert seamstresses, because if there are holes between stitches, everyone dies of frostbite. Their sewing bags are made from caribou leg skin and filled with needles, whittled from the animal's bones and antlers, and thread made from its sinew.

LUMBERSEXUAL

While this trend hit NYC and LA a few years back, lumberjack chic is a way of life in these parts. Fads come and go, but a sweaty, rugged mountain man will lurk in the Great Plains forever. Here's how to nail the look, even if you can't chop down a tree to save your life.

FLANNEL FAB

Before Kurt Cobain made flannel a mandatory grunge accessory, the Welsh developed the fabric, calling upon their large sheep population for wool. In 1889, flannel came to 'Merica via a Detroit factory, producing the stuff to keep workers warm. This isn't your thin wannabe flannel. To be true to lumberjack style, your flannel needs to be thick cotton and breathable so you can swing that axe with ease. It'll need to handle at least three layers under it and five layers over it.

WORK THE BOOTS

You'll need some waterproof boots that hold up in snow and mud and won't give you blisters, because there is nothing sexy about blisters. While Timberland (you know, like lumber but timber?) and (scoff) L.L. Bean make popular ones, a German immigrant is responsible for the introduction of rugged footwear to the United States. Peter Weinbrenner opened his boot-making factory in Milwaukee in 1855, and the company—the oldest made-in-the-USA boot brand—buddied up to the Industrial Revolution to innovate job-specific styles.

OTP Tip: A durable pair of sweat-wicking socks is key to looking like Paul Bunyon, sans actual bunions.

WOOL PANTS

Why wool? Well, it has to do with odors. Nothing quite says lumberjack whack like ball sweat. Real lumberjacks and loggers lived near bodies of water for ease of transport once they cut down something massive. In addition to the sweat you built up climbing, hacking, and competing in log-rolling competitions, surrounding humidity can make for some smelly conditions down south. Wool is a natural odor-trapper and is great at absorbing moisture and dispersing it through the air; and while it's itchy, wool is breathable.

EARFLAP CAP

A lumberjack's cap is a five-panel contraption with earflaps. You fold and tie them up when you're casually strolling around town, and pull those earflaps out when it's time to get down to business. Its style comes from an *ushanka*, that furry Russian hat worn by soldiers to keep the cold weather from freezing their ears. Lumberjack hats are made out of more practical materials and also work to dampen the sound of noisy chain saws.

LET'S TALK BEARDS

Beards are, essentially, a face blanket. So when you're walking around Brooklyn in the humid heat of August and dudes be like, "What? I can't shave it. It's part of my look," you begin to wonder how the fuck the beard got taken so far out of context. The beard—together with your ability to grow and groom it—is the ultimate symbol of manliness that's icing on the man cake if you're an actual lumberjack, and a hairy layer of facial mystery if you're not. If you're taking your beard out of the forest and want to get near other faces, the trick is keeping the beast at bay with beard oil. Extra points if you can get it to smell like vanilla custard.

BONUS

POWER TOOL OF CHOICE

Accessorizing with a toolbelt is totally optional. For a city dweller, we suggest a power drill if you're going for a *Home Improvement* look, and a chain saw if mountain murderer is how you roll.

HOARDER MUSEUMS ACROSS 'MERICA!

We all have our moments of holding onto something for sentimental reasons or collecting strange items for the hell of it. But these five people have taken the nostalgia thing to a whole new level. It turns out that some collections are totally wacky, including everything from toilet seats to pickled tumors.

BELHAVEN MEMORIAL MUSEUM, BELHAVEN, NORTH CAROLINA

Here, you can find the personal collection of Mrs. Evan Blount Way, who died at ninety-two in 1964, and loved weird-ass shit like jarred pig fetuses, pickled tumors, and a half boot from World War II that came off along with whatever foot was inside it.

SALT & PEPPER SHAKER MUSEUM, GATLINBURG, TENNESSEE

And you thought your grandma's pantry was ridiculous? This place is packed with over twenty thousand salt and pepper shakers made from various materials and shaped like everything from vegetables to Obama.

BARNEY SMITH'S TOILET SEAT ART MUSEUM, SAN ANTONIO, TEXAS

Barney Smith was a plumber and found his true calling after retirement. For more than fifty years, Barney's been doodling portraits, gluing knick-knacks (like handles from a coffin Barney found in his yard), and creating masterpieces of sorts atop toilet seats, the most unlikely of canvases.

TRUNDLE MANOR, SWISSVALE, PENNSYLVANIA

A gathering of every morbid thing you can possibly imagine, the Manor is a house built in 1910 that the Addams Family would be happy to occupy, complete with a jarred frog, a magnified human tumor, and deer fetuses floating in (maybe) urine.

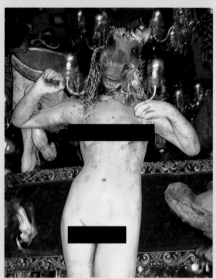

HOUSE ON THE ROCK, SPRING GREEN, WISCONSIN

The high-up house didn't stop eccentric artist Alex Jordan Jr. from hauling all kinds of crazy shit inside, like suits of armor, model airplanes, pipe organs, string instruments, and fiberglass elephants.

FEEDSACK FASHIONS

Nebraska has always had more chickens, cows, and pigs roaming around than any other state. During the Great Depression, sacks left over from holding livestock feed, along with grains, flour, and sugar, were repurposed into feedsack fashions. They had to make do with what they had, and what they made was a bold, utilitarian fashion statement.

BOX TO BAG

Originally, the packaging for food staples consisted of mostly barrels, tins, or crates, which would not be ideal for long-term storage, as they tended to leak or rust. In the 1800s, bags, mostly made of canvas or cotton, made an appearance. During this time, the new cloth coming into farm households started to be repurposed for clothing, quilts, and other household items.

When the country's economy rebounded, this practice fell out of favor. But once the Depression hit in the '30s, women returned to using and reusing everything, and bags were made into dresses once again. Since World War II uniforms sucked up the fabrics on the market, farm women used what was available to them to create household items. Since many of the bags were identical, women began showing off their sewing skills to create distinctive designs, often mimicking fashionable dresses using only feedsacks.

Women became artisans, and since they participated in the economy of the home, they had a say in which feedsacks their husbands purchased. Creating something out of waste gave women a sense of pride and earned them respect.

COLORFUL SACKS

Once manufacturers caught wind that women were using bags as clothes (and as towels, curtains, and anything that required fabric, really) and choosing the most patterned and colorful bags to make things less drab, feedsack bags were manufactured to be more creative and aesthetically pleasing, with printed patterns and designs.

Now, this wasn't because big business wanted to make school kids feel like they were wearing actual cool clothes. It was free advertising. The minute bags became less cost-effective, as new paper and plastic packaging hit the market, manufacturers dropped the canvas and moms across the Midwest had to look for other means of keeping their kids from going to school naked. Chances are if you ask middle-aged Midwesterners about what they wore to school, it'll bring back some tearful memories.

HORSE FASHIONS

The Plains Indians are a decorated bunch, and not just for fashion purposes, and not just the people. Plains horses were fitted with masks in battle to channel the spirit of the hides they had on their faces. The intricately designed masks of these fashion-forward equestrian warriors make whatever you're wearing right now look like horseshit.

HORSE-STORY

The first horses acquired by Native Americans came from the Spanish. Plains Indians are a mobile culture, and every material thing they have or make must serve a practical purpose. Blackfeet horse masks were light but intricately designed pieces, inspired by Spanish armor. The masks were made to resemble buffalo heads, and the equestrians who controlled the horses wearing them garnered respect. Horses changed the game for the Native Americans of the Plains. They allowed them to hunt more buffalo and wield sheer power and strength. Decorating them in glorious horse fashions made a lot of sense.

RAW MATERIALS

While the masks often obscured the vision of horses, they were damn pretty and took a lot of artsy work to put together. Oftentimes made from ermine (a tiny weasel native to the region), buffalo horns, brass belts, porcupine quillwork, feathers, hides, fabric, beads, and dyed horse hair, the masks displayed the finest of Native American craftsmanship. In addition to masks, horses were outfitted in handmade saddles, bridles, whips, and ropes. The masks were also made to be taken apart and used in pieces. For instance, the area around the cheeks would later be used as a pipe bag, and the lower neck section would be repurposed into moccasins. Until this day, horses sport their sassy masks in parades and events on the Great Plains.

THE SPIRIT OF THE SCALP

These horse masks gave new meaning to spirit animals. Not only were buffalo hides placed on horse faces considered a way of channeling the spirit of the larger animal, but the decorative elements around the eyes were said to call upon the Thunder Beings. Known as *Wakinyan* to the Lakota people of the Black Hills, Thunder Beings were associated with thunder, lightning, and storms, and were said to bring both life and destruction. The Thunderbird was a powerful symbolic creature whose voice was thunder. Lightning flashed from the Thunderbird's eyes, and the Plains Indians evoked this symbol on the eyes of horse masks, with glass beads and reflective materials.

WINNER WINNER TV DINNER

Food used to be served at the dinner table. Dad worked, Mom cooked, you ate, and you didn't complain. While this may be an outdated (and sexist) idea of the nuclear American family, it was how dinner went down every night. The TV dinner, with its shiny tray and lure of freedom from drudgery in the kitchen, changed everything. Each compartment held the promise of feeding your family without being tied to the stove. Plus, the trusty trash did the dishes.

MAIN

The first frozen individual meal was developed in 1941 and was utilized in the military and on airplanes, settings where eating alone and quickly were a necessity. Several companies played around with the idea, and by the '50s, the sale of frozen dinners picked up steam. In 1954, Swanson—a Nebraska company with its hands deep in the turkey, egg, and dairy industries—rebranded frozen meals and tied them to the TV.

Some say Swanson was sitting on a bunch of old turkey and needed a way to push it out to the public, and, sure enough, the first dinner was turkey with cornbread dressing, sweet potatoes, and frozen peas. With a nudge from Swanson, dinner effectively moved from the table and onto people's laps, in front of the TV. The confluence of TV's growing popularity pulled frozen dinners with it, and Swanson sold ten million TV dinners in 1954 alone.

Fun Fact
The original Swanson metal TV dinner tray is on display at the Smithsonian National Museum of American History in D.C.

SIDE

On the one side, TV dinners came on the 'Merican scene at a time when women began to find jobs outside the home. Since women were still tied to the kitchen, this meant that there was a need for faster-cooking meals. When women were unshackled from the stove, the single man became the prime target for frozen dinners. Swanson was eventually acquired by Pinnacle Foods, which rebranded the dinners as Hungry Man meals. Pinnacle refocused the target demographic, appealing to the single, can't-cook-for-shit, dude.

OTHER SIDE

With their compartments and mystery meats, TV dinners diluted the connection between people and food. Eating became

a solitary act with your friends on the tube. Swanson found foods that cooked for the same amount of time, further disconnecting people from culinary know-how. Convenience became king and eating became mindless.

THE TV PART

Ad men knew you were watching TV while dipping your fork into overcooked green beans and lumpy mashed potatoes. Commercials were made to show you that something tastier (fast food) was just as easy to shovel into your mouth, plus you didn't even have to "cook" it as you did TV

dinners. Swanson's downfall came when TV dinners weren't competing just with home-cooking, but also with take-out restaurant meals. Fast food won the battle of who got America's food dollars, and 'Mericans began a winner-less battle with the bulge.

FAMOUS FLAVORS

While TV dinners started as simple compositions of familiar, all-American favorites that paired meat, potatoes, and some sort of vegetable (usually carrots and peas), some companies began differentiating themselves by offering new foods and tastes of "international" cuisine. When Americans had their fill of sliced beef and such, potpies began hitting the freezer aisle, along with German-style meals (the same American stuff but with a weirder gravy), and of course, the full-on Thanksgiving dinner, which symbolized that Americans just gave up on eating with other people for a while.

=== *Fun Fact* ===

In 2008, you could get a $30 TV dinner at the Loews Regency Hotel in New York, with options such as free-range fried chicken, cheddar and Asiago mac 'n' cheese, and Burgundian pinot noir braised pot roast.

ONLY IN . . .

While many 'Merican creations gained traction all around the country, these foods remained confined to their hometowns and are only available here. Are they good? That's up for debate. But they do speak to the hearts of the locals who love them.

ST. PAUL SANDWICH, MISSOURI

A strange blend of Chinese food between two slices of white bread, the St. Paul was created in the '40s by Chinese restaurants pandering to 'Merica's love of sandwiches. What's in it? An egg foo young patty topped with your typical burger accoutrements.

CHOW MEIN SANDWICH, MASSACHUSETTS/RHODE ISLAND

Similar to the St. Paul, except with more carbs than you'll ever want in one meal, the popular noodle dish gets doused in brown gravy and shoved inside a hamburger bun. It's messy, impractical, and completely ridiculous.

DUTCH CRUNCH, SAN FRANCISCO, CALIFORNIA

It looks like crispy giraffe skin, and outside of the Bay Area not a single sandwich in America will ever feel the warm hug of Dutch crunch bread. Outside of the States, the Netherlands sells "tiger bread" and the UK has "giraffe bread."

PEPPERONI ROLLS, WEST VIRGINIA

Invented in 1927, this is West Virginia's glorified hot pocket and consists of a yeasty white roll, stuffed with pepperoni and warmed until the

meat fat fuses with the bread, creating an I'll-work-out-later kind of snack.

GOETTA, OHIO

A mush made with meat and oats, the Goetta originated in Germany and stuck around the Cincinnati area. The oats serve as a way to beef up the meat, making a more filling meal from scraps.

CUDIGHI, MICHIGAN

This came from Northern Italy and settled in Michigan, where it turned into a regional favorite that consists of spiced, flattened sausage drenched in mozzarella and pizza sauce.

SLINGER, MISSOURI

Order one of these bad boys and prepare to be wowed by how little the Midwest cares about the presentation of food. A mishmash of eggs, meat, chili, and cheese, the Slinger has many variations (sometimes with a tamale on top), but one thing always remains the same: It must look like a gooey pile of regret.

BEER CHEESE SOUP, WISCONSIN

Of course Wisconsin would have a soup loaded with beer and cheese. You can get this in Germany, but Wisconsin's version comes with a side of cheesehead pride.

MEAT AND POTATOES

Meat and potatoes are the bread and butter of the Northwest. Sure, vegetables might find their way into people's bellies from time to time, but this land is brimming with the heavier foodstuffs. Idaho is synonymous with potatoes, and Nebraska is the king of steak. The two come together to create hearty regional dishes with all-American flair.

MEAT

Omaha is the undisputed champ of huge, monstrous steaks. Surrounded by grazing lands, it is no surprise that this town owns it when it comes to cow. The smell of manure leads the way to Omaha, and once you hit the town that was built on beef, signs and cow sculptures let you know that you're in beef heaven.

It started back in 1883 with the Omaha Stockyards, which opened as a location for cow processing closer to the West than plants in places like Chicago. By the 1960s, the stockyards were the middleman, and packers started dealing directly with ranchers for quicker processing, effectively putting the stockyards out of business by 1999.

During its heyday, though, Omaha's meat-centric restaurant scene boomed, with steakhouses searing mountains of meat every day, and Omaha Steaks, a mail-order beef distributor, spreading its products across the country. Eating in Omaha today means that even if you order chicken, you'll get it sauced with beef drippings. It's just the Omaha way.

=== *Fun Fact* ===

While New Yorkers will punch you in the face if you ever bring it up, the iconic Reuben sandwich is said to have originated in Omaha.

POTATOES

Idaho has more potato power than any other state in 'Merica, producing 30 percent of the country's spud supply. How did this place turn into tuber town? Idaho has the perfect growing conditions for potatoes: warm days, cool nights, and fertile soil deposited by the Snake River. Henry Spalding planted the first Idaho potato in 1837, and today, about thirteen billion pounds of potatoes are produced in the state. While many varieties grow here, it is the humble Russet Burbank that gave Idaho its potato fame. Russets are smooth-fleshed, have a long storage life, and have the right moisture content to create French fries, the food that has fueled Idaho's $2 billion potato industry since the '50s.

MEAT AND POTATOES

Meat and potatoes are great on their own, but combine the two and you have unique regional dishes that can satisfy the hearty appetites of the Great Plains. Here are three to sink your teeth into.

Hot Dish

Like tater tots that put on a fat suit and hopped in the oven, this popular casserole is a combo of tots, ground beef, canned vegetables, and canned soup. The hot dish makes frequent guest appearances at communal gatherings and festivals.

Cornish Pasty

A handheld pastry pouch containing potatoes, swedes (rutabaga), onions, and beef, the Cornish pasty originated in Cornwall, England, and was introduced to the Northwestern states through European miners. While its origins might be international, this portable meat-and-potato treat is revered in colder Northern states.

Jucy Lucy with Fries

This is a burger where cheese makes an appearance twice—inside the actual beef patty and on top. Two bars in Minneapolis claim they invented the Lucy, with one spelling it *Juicy* and the other leaving out the *i* to differentiate it from the competition. Either way, the Ju(i)cy Lucy is best eaten with fries to soak up the remaining drippings.

OTP Tip: The Runza sandwich—a long pastry filled with beef and cabbage—is somewhat of a gluttonous delicacy here.

EAT LIKE A NORTH DAKOTA VIKING

North America's largest Scandinavian festival, the Norsk Høstfest goes down in Minot, North Dakota (of all places), every year in the fall. Lasting five full days, the fest covers an array of cultures, including Iceland, Norway, Sweden, Denmark, and Finland. We guarantee you'll be weirded out by 90 percent of the stuff here, but fear not: We're here to explain all the strange bits so you can chow down with the rest of the proud Nordic North Dakotans.

SMORGASBORD

North Dakotans don't mess with tasting menus and individual courses; instead, food is usually served family style with many little dishes that all mingle on your plate. The Norsk Høstfest is family style on a grand scale with funky food, good tunes, culinary demonstrations, troll beauty contests, award ceremonies, and a full-on Viking village, with steel combat performances, art, and jewelry. Bring your horned hat and fill it with both traditional and totally-messed-with Nordic foods at the fest.

Lefse

The premier food item of the fest, Lefse is Norway's answer to the tortilla. A crepelike flatbread, Lefse is made from potatoes, cream, and butter, then served with more butter and a bit of sugar. While traditionally Lefse is eaten as is, Americans have put a lovely spin on the dish by stuffing it with peanut butter or wrapping it around hot dogs.

OTP Tip: If you can roll out the boiled potatoes like it's nobody's business, consider competing at the festival for the Master of Lefse title.

Lutefisk

This is "aged" (aka rotten) whitefish that's been treated with lye and air-dried for days until it achieves a gelatinous texture. It's an acquired taste and has been toned down a bit for American tastes; nonetheless, if you're squeamish about smelly fish, this one's going to be putrid.

Viking on a Stick

A friendly blend of giant meatball and corn dog, this one is meant to unhinge your jaw. If we're being honest, we'd prefer a skewered Viking, in all his sweaty, hairy glory, over rotten fish any day.

Swedish Meatballs

Are they just like the ones you get in Ikea? Yup. But outside, and near Vikings.

Oof-Da Tacos

We've tasted every mangled variation of tacos all across 'Merica, but this one takes the taco cake. *Uff da* is a Scandinavian expression that loosely translates to "I'm overwhelmed," and this traveling taco stand reflects the term well. The shell is fry bread, instead of a tortilla, that's topped with Taco Bell–quality fixin's (plus sliced olives). We're not sure what these have to do with Scandinavia, but eating one of these is guaranteed to make Pancho Villa roll over in his grave.

Aebleskivers

A Danish creation, these are little sweet greaseballs prepared in their own special pan, with little spherical indentations. They start out as typical pancake batter, but with more dairy, which is then poured in the pan and turned with a knitting needle to create balls that are firm on the outside and fluffy in the middle.

Rømmegrøt

It's porridge loaded with dairy in the form of heavy sour cream that is then drizzled with butter, sprinkled with cinnamon and sugar, and oddly eaten as a side dish to meat. For something sweeter and more familiar, the fest also has bread pudding.

I CAN SEE RUSSIA: PELMENI IN ALASKA

While she was governor of Alaska, Sarah Palin likely gobbled some Russian eats, as the state is apparently so close to Mother Russia that Sarah sees it from her house. Well, it may not be *that* close, Mrs. Palin, but this former Russian territory did leave a delicious impression on 'Merica's iciest state.

While you can get an array of food in the Russian enclaves of Brooklyn's Brighton Beach and LA's West Hollywood, Alaska offers an interesting Americanized version of Russia's most comforting food (next to vodka).

WHO DUMPED THE DUMPLINGS?

Americans are familiar with all kinds of dumplings, mostly from Asia. Even Polish pierogi are more popular than their Russian dumpling brothers. Proximity and history make Alaska the only state that's truly up on its pelmeni game.

It all started with fur and a Russian man named Grigory Shelikhov, who founded Three Saints Bay on Kodiak Island; he lived there with his wife and two hundred men for a few days until he needed to go back to the motherland for borscht and pickle-backs. The Russians made some half-assed attempts at keeping Alaska for themselves,

but eventually the United States put up some green to get them off the ice. But everyone knows Russians don't just go away without a trace; Russian cuisine still lingers where the sun don't shine.

===== *Fun Fact* =====

President Andrew Jackson was mocked for what people believed was a frivolous purchase, calling Alaska his "polar bear garden." Until gold was discovered in Alaska; then everyone promptly proceeded to shut the fuck up.

PELMENI?
I BARELY KNOW HER

Pelmeni are delicate balls of dough, stuffed with flavorful, juicy ground chicken or pork, lightly boiled, and served with regionally specific condiments. In Russia, the farther north you go, the heartier your pelmeni get.

Down in Ukraine, a splash of vinegar, a dash of pepper, and a pat of butter will do; up north in St. Petersburg, the meat purses are doused in butter and covered with a blanket of cheese. In Alaska, things like beef find their way inside the dumpling, and toppings never seen in the motherland (like cilantro and sriracha) are mixed in. Other Russian remixes, like blini (eaten with caviar traditionally), are topped with crabmeat in Alaska. Speaking of which . . .

TRUE BLUE
ALASKAN DISHES

While Russia plays a part in flavoring Alaskan cuisine, the surrounding waters are where the dinner lives. Populated first by the Inuit, Alaska thrives on catch-and-bake food like crab and fish, which are established staples. Crab here is so good it'll make you want to shoot a wolf from a helicopter.

But if you really want to chew the fat of native Alaskan cuisine, you must sample *pemmican*, which is essentially a meat pie with dried berries, made primarily from animal fat. And for dessert? We've got just the thing. Eskimo ice cream—a loose paste of whipped seal or bear fat mixed with berries and ice (and zero sugar)—is like a trip to the slushie machine with a stop at the Dumpster.

MUSIC

HOW TO POWWOW

Like musical theater but with deep cultural roots, the powwow is a party with a purpose. In the Great Plains region, powwows happen often. There's one on the Fourth of July, Thanksgiving, Harvest Festival, and all kinds of other dates on the calendar year-round. If you feel like powwing, chances are there's a powwow going on right now.

POW PARTY

The *pau-wau* started as a healing ceremony, said to have originated with the Pawnee tribe that resided along the North Platte River in Nebraska. Powwows evolved to celebrate successful hunts and harvests, to honor various spirits, and to prepare warriors for battle. Powwows were crucial to disseminating oral history through interpretive dance and storytelling and were traditionally tribe-specific.

Today, the party maintains some of its cultural roots with drum circles, dancing, and plenty of feathers, but also includes Indian taco stands, a befuddling idea that swaps tortillas for fry bread (a sour milk-leavened dough that's deep-fried in oil, shortening, or lard).

=== *Fun(ish) Fact* ===

Women were not traditionally allowed at powwows, but since the population of Native Americans has declined so much, not only are they welcome but various tribes join together to throw a proper party that includes both sexes.

DRESS

If you're going to wow anybody at the pow, you should probably wear whatever you're wearing right now. Unless you're part of the tribe, you have to be conscious of being a respectful spectator. That said, you're going to see some really cool shit. People dress to reflect their community, their individuality, their history, and elements of modern life.

While you'll see feathers, incredible beadwork, masks, and animal hides, you'll also see things like Disney character barrettes and beads. Regalia is like a collage you wear of your life, adding a piece for every significant event; regalia also varies depending on the dance you're doing.

OTP Tip: Never call these outfits "costumes" unless you want a swift kick in the feathers. The proper term is *regalia*.

DRUM AND DANCE

Prepare for things to get loud—and not that thumping festival bass loud, but the pounding of numerous drums loud. The drum is said to represent the heartbeat of the Native American nation and is believed to bring the disjointed people's physical and mental states of being back together through rhythm.

While there are a number of drums at a powwow, a central drum, played by a group of people and made out of buffalo (or other animal) hide keeps the heartbeat going. Dancing around the drumming is specifically divided by gender and purpose. Northern traditional dancing involves elaborate headdresses made of porcupine and deer hair; many accessories crafted from bones, hides, and bells; and one row of distinctive tail feathers. The dancer here mimicks a pecking chicken and symbolizes a warrior in search of his enemy.

Powwows have become educational events that teach community members about Native American traditions and spectators are welcome. Just don't go around touching a guy's drum; that's a big powwow no-no.

MAHA MUSIC FESTIVAL

Aside from manhandling your weight in steak, the most exciting thing you can do in Omaha, Nebraska, is the Maha Music Festival. While you'd expect any fest in Nebraska to be overrun by cowboy hats and country tunes, this one's not for the ranchers. Maha is a nonprofit music festival; tickets are only $50 and give you access to good jams for a full twelve hours during the mild summer days of August.

THE SCENE

The fest takes place in the park at Aksarben Village, a fabricated community that's a little too clean to be cool, but the fest-goers punk it up a bit. The music blares from two stages and the park is small, which is kind of nice because you don't need to go to the music; it comes to you.

The event is for all ages so you might mosh a toddler, but the crowd tends to skew high school. We love festivals, but one thing they never get right is the bathroom situation. Here, it's pretty luxurious, with two dedicated porta-potty villages operated by volunteers to keep things moving.

OTP Tip: You fancy yourself a king? For a fancy throne, VIPs get access to deluxe porta-potties with flushable toilets, running water, and air-conditioning.

THE MUSIC

While the most famous person to ever come out of Omaha has to be Marlon Brando (maybe Warren Buffett), the fest attracts some great artists to the city. Maha starts slow, with local acts taking the stage earlier in the day, and builds as the sun sets.

The local bands have hard-core fan bases and the energy grips the crowd even before anyone you've ever heard of hits the stage. Closing acts tend to be major national bands like Delta Spirit and beloved bands like Garbage. While eight thousand to ten thousand people gather each year

at Maha, the venue is more intimate, which means the artists get more personal.

THE FOOD

You can choose a liquid diet for twelve hours, but chances are you'll need something to munch on. In addition to the brick-and-mortar restaurants in the surrounding Aksarben Village, vendors at the festival offer a range of edibles from sushi to pizza, and set up in trucks and tents around the event. Local favorites like Big Daddy's Donuts, Voodoo Taco, and Dante's Pizzeria make sure you're not running on just Omaha air. The vendors' vegan and vegetarian offerings are clearly denoted for those who need a break from steak.

TESTY FESTY

The Testy Festy in Clinton, Montana, is a celebration of "Rocky Mountain oysters" or delicious animal testicles, complete with strippers, balls, and all kinds of madness. While outside of Montana (Florida not included), wet T-shirt contests seem like a barbaric, shameful part of our collective past, the Testy Festy has four separate contests to make sure every feminist is more pissed than a raging bull. No one under twenty is allowed because everyone turns into a naked, ball-loving drunk by the end of the fest. The entire celebration is so high on testosterone you'll have to swallow your weight in bull balls to keep up. Here are some of the highlights.

TESTY CONTEST

What do you do when there's an over-whelming surplus of bull balls bouncing around? Shove them in your mouth in less than four minutes to win prizes, of course! They're sliced, battered, and fried so it's not quite so bad, but still bad enough to barf. You wanna chase it down with ranch? They got it. The Rock Creek Lodge in Clinton serves several tons of these bad boys every year. Expect running jokes about balls and innuendo of the elementary school variety.

> ===== *Fun Fact* =====
>
> Byron, Illinois, has the oldest testicle festival in the country and features turkey balls.

UNDIE 500

The Undie 500 is a combo of tricycles and people in underwear. Some people go for full frontal, while others tuck their testes in tight for the ride. The extra stability offered by the tricycle is welcome after a day of eating gonads with ranch dressing and washing it all down with buckets of whiskey and beer.

It's not about winning the race—it's about being as obnoxious as possible.

BIG BALL CONTEST

You didn't think you could walk out of this place without dropping your pants, now did you? For the Big Ball Contest, you get up onstage, drop your pants, and let the women folk inspect your goods. The biggest, best-formed, most perfumed testicles win the Big Ball Contest. The little lumpy balls can always try again next year.

Montana isn't the only place crawling with balls; many other places across the country hold small festivals to get rid of their extra animal testicles. While they're called calf frys in Oklahoma and lamb fries elsewhere, going down they're all the same.

> ===== *Fun Fact* =====
>
> Testicle festivals aren't limited to 'Merica. Every September, Serbia hosts The World Testicle Cooking Championships (or Ballcup), where a slew of competitors cross their swords to cook an array of animal balls from ostrich to kangaroo to swan.

STURGIS MOTORCYCLE RALLY

The culture surrounding motorcycles sprang from post–World War II when veterans searched for the same bromances, thrills, and fast-moving excitement that they'd had in the war. The motorcycle is a symbol of freedom. It's just you, some under-crotch horsepower, and the open road. From race cars to minivans, 'Merica loves its vehicles, and big, fat Harleys roll in their own class. Every August, the Black Hills National Forest of South Dakota blows up with the sound of Harley exhaust and the biker dudes and babes who love 'em.

RALLY!

Started in 1936 by Pappy Hoel, the rally has been around for more than seventy-five years and reels an astonishing half million people into South Dakota every year. Some make cross-country rides on their bikes, with international motorcycle enthusiasts appearing as well. Imagine the front of a biker bar on a Sunday afternoon, multiply that by ten thousand, and add scenic roads, competitions, dazzling leathers, and vendors, and you'll begin to understand the madness of Sturgis.

While a large chunk of riders still favor chrome-and-leather Harleys, the welcoming of sports bikes and dirty, dirty mountain racers lure younger bikers into the mix. It started as a competitive event, but many people go just to ride through the Black Hills and the Badlands, by the faces of Mount Rushmore, and around the little towns.

OTP Tip: If shit gets too wild to handle, there's a silo and fallout shelter nearby that can send a missile to the "Soviet Union" (because they don't know it's completely dissolved now?) in thirty minutes.

GEAR AND INK

The Rally is littered with an array of vendors. You can stock up on accessories, like hats, gloves, jackets, and the kind of T-shirts your dad will want to borrow. You can also pimp out your bike here with pro shops set up to cater to every biker's need. Want to get a tattoo you'll regret? There's enough beer and booze here to lube yourself up before hitting one of Sturgis's tattoo shops. Buffalo Bills Tattoo Emporium has been poking thick skin for years, and can decorate yours with the biker babe of your dreams.

PARTY LIKE A BIKER

At saloons around town, people like Bret Michaels and others with long locks make musical appearances to stir the crowd. The main event, though, is the giant Buf-

falo Chip outdoor stage, where for ten days, acts like Lynyrd Skynyrd, Def Leppard, and Social Distortion entertain the massive crowds of bald, bearded, and leathered bikers. Here, you can watch the bikers roll in swarms, catch stunt shows, pursue motorcycle-centric art exhibits, and get some oh-so-politically-incorrect midget bowling under your belt. Plus, every year, a new Miss Buffalo Chip biker babe is crowned onstage wearing close to nothing. Will there be a bunch of dirty middle-aged men there? You betcha.

BUFFALO ROUNDUP

If you stay through September, the engines cool off and the bison heat up. Custer Park in South Dakota is home to the world's largest bison herd at thirteen hundred strong. During the roundup, cowboys and cowgirls saddle up and encircle the herd to create a thundering, thumping spectacle of hooves and mayhem. If you prefer bison-power to horsepower, this is a must-see event.

CHEYENNE FRONTIER DAYS

For more than one hundred years, Cheyenne, Wyoming, has been throwing a bronco-bucking, rope-twirling, cattle-canoodling party where the baddest cowboys come out to celebrate the culture of the Northwest. Immerse yourself in this ten-day, midsummer festival where the gunslingers are grand and the cowgirls are always sassy. This is the world's biggest rodeo and you can't leave until you're properly branded and smell like manure.

SADDLE UP!

Started as a one-day event in 1897, the Cheyenne Frontier Days kept growing with age. After over one hundred years, this thing is the biggest bovine blowout in the world. The rodeo goes down in a nineteen-thousand-seat stadium that's packed with screaming cowboy lovers, and this isn't just for fun. The cash and prizes run up to $1 million, so people are in it to win it. The events showcase an array of cowboy skills, like roping, steer wrestling, bareback riding, and barrel racing.

Ranch sorting is an event where two cowboys are pitted against marked cows that they must sort into their correct pens. The big event is the bull-riding competition, where an experienced cowboy gets his crotch mangled by a pissed-off bull for the chance to win $100,000 and the championship title.

OTP Tip: If you like your bull sans buck, the Frontier Days also feature the Grand Parade, where tractors roll down the street for as far as the eye can see and the hottest farm equipment gets its time to shine.

COWBOY COOKIN'

Cowboys are the pioneers of food trucks and we all know everything tastes better out of a streetside window. Along with carnival food served throughout the fest, the chuck wagons here hold three free

pancake breakfasts where 5,000 pounds of pancake mix, 630 pounds of butter, and 3,000 pounds of ham are gobbled up by ravenously hungry festgoers every year. What's more, the chuck-wagon cook-off is a culinary spectacle where cowboys are given a limited set of tools and ingredients and are challenged to create amazing meals.

COUNTRY SHOWS

The Frontier Days give you an opportunity to party with several guys named Keith and sometimes Aerosmith. Concerts are held every night around town and feature someone in a cowboy hat or at least boots with spurs. There is also an air show put on by the U.S. Air Force Thunderbirds; Native American demonstrations in the Indian Village; and a fair with rides, games, and the kind of artery-clogging barbecue you'd expect. The daddy of 'em all, the Cheyenne Frontier Days pack 200,000 people into the multifaceted event every year, with people looking for lodging overflowing Wyoming's borders into Colorado and Nebraska.

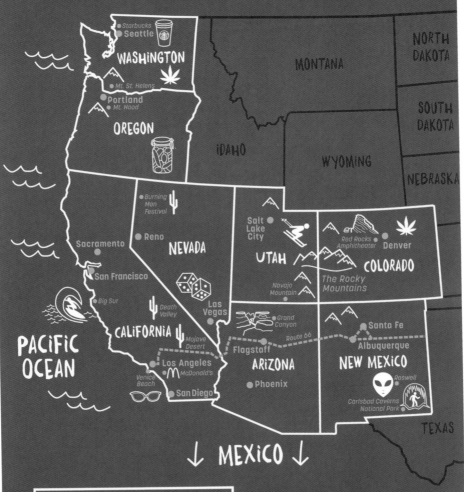

↑ CANADA ↑

NORTH DAKOTA

MONTANA

WASHINGTON

● Starbucks
● Seattle

● Mt. St. Helens
● Portland
● Mt. Hood

OREGON

IDAHO

SOUTH DAKOTA

WYOMING

NEBRASKA

Burning Man Festival

● Reno

NEVADA

Sacramento ●

San Francisco ●

Big Sur ●

Death Valley

CALIFORNIA

Mojave Desert

Los Angeles ●
Venice Beach ●
McDonald's

San Diego ●

Salt Lake City ●

UTAH

Navajo Mountain

Las Vegas ●

Grand Canyon

Flagstaff ●

ARIZONA

Phoenix ●

Red Rocks Amphitheater ●

Denver ●

COLORADO

The Rocky Mountains

Route 66

Santa Fe ●
Albuquerque ●

NEW MEXICO

Roswell ●

Carlsbad Caverns National Park ●

TEXAS

PACIFIC OCEAN

↓ MEXICO ↓

PACIFIC OCEAN

HAWAii

THE GODDAMN HIPPIES

The West is a place where rebels went to escape governing bodies, to stake out their own fates and stick it to the man from afar. The West's canyons and ocean-fronted cliffs, plus milder weather, are perfect for really falling in love with the outdoors. Get lost in Oregon's forests, get thirsty in the Mojave Desert, and wash away your worries in the Pacific along the California coast. If big cities are more your thing, hype up on coffee in Seattle, eat your weight in fussy food in Portland, try your hand at acting as an extra in LA, and finish it off with a cold one in Denver, the city where beer is holy water.

WHAT THE F*CK IS SANDBOARDING?

We all know that you can throw a board on cement, snow, or the ocean, but have you ever considered dropping in on some sand? Out in the dune-filled desert, sandboarding is a thing. A thing that'll fill every crevice of your body with tiny grains of sand in the name of thrills.

SANDY LOGISTICS

Sandboarding was revived in the '40s, but it goes back to ancient Egypt. Hiking to the top of a dune, with your legs throbbing, and panting for air is like that feeling you get when you find a snow-packed hill by the highway and slide down atop a trash-can lid, but with more sand and fewer tree branches getting in your way. The fun here lies in the changing landscape. Dunes are always worked by the weather and the changing positions of the sun turn the desert kaleidoscope just a click every hour.

WHERE THERE'S A DUNE, THERE'S A WAY

The world is filled with dunes, and this part of 'Merica's desert landscape is no exception. Huge, rolling dunes cover many parts of the West and these five are the best for gliding to your heart's content.

Colorado

The Great Sand Dunes National Park and Preserve has the tallest dunes in the country, surrounded by grasslands, wetlands, and aspen forests. Sandboarding here is

best for early birds because the sand heats up to 150 degrees once the sun has been up for some time.

Arizona

The Hot Well Dunes get their name from a well that produces 250 gallons of water per minute. Here, the fun lies in hiking up the big dune and dropping, avoiding ATVs, dirt bikes, and shrubbery on your way down. The area's soaking tubs are great for getting the sandboarding-inflicted kinks out.

Utah

Boarding down the Coral Pink Sand Dunes will feel like planting your feet on Mars. The sand is made up of mountain particles and the three thousand acres of sand form dunes 300 to 350 feet tall. Hit these at dusk when the sunset gives the coral pink sand a golden glow.

California

The Kelso Dunes in the Mojave Desert reach a towering six hundred feet and are reserved for sandboarders, with no ATVs allowed. This sand oasis is made up of pink feldspar that provides a colorful background for when you fall over yourself and eat sand.

Oregon

The Sand Master Park is the world's first sand park. Here, you'll find dunes, bowls, cliffs, advanced slopes, rail slides, and a forty-foot-long cushioned ramp, all set against the Oregon Rain Forest. The Sand Master Jam, when the pros show off their sandboarding skills, goes down on the third weekend of July.

OTP Tip: If you can make it out to Hawaii, you'll have plenty to board on. They even add a little kite to your sandboard for a next-level fusion adventure.

THE SPOOKIEST GHOST TOWNS IN 'MERICA

Even if you cried fearful tears every time an episode of *X-Files* came on, there's something about ghost towns that draw people in. There's nothing to do; nothing to see. Yet, we can't resist stopping by to imagine the life that once was and why it ended. Lucky for you, the pursuit of the American Dream sometimes leads to complete failure. From the dried-up gold mines in the West to the shut-down Industrial Revolution towns of the East, these are the most beautiful, spooky, desolate ghost towns around the country.

CALICO, YERMO, CALIFORNIA

Between Vegas and LA, Calico might first seem like a mirage in the desert, but we assure you it's real. You already know about the Gold Rush, but there was a short-lived silver rush in California when the shiny stuff was discovered there in the late 1800s. Calico was populated by those hungry for silver who couldn't quite get a bite of gold. When the town's ore lost its glimmer and the price of silver didn't hold up the way gold did, people fled and left behind this mine-filled relic of a town. For decades, it stood in disrepair, falling apart gracefully at the seams until *Aaar*nold declared it a landmark in 2005, giving it a proper tourist face-lift.

OTP Tip: You'll know that you're close when you see the "Zzyzyx" exit—the best use of the last letters of the alphabet, in our opinion.

PICHER, OKLAHOMA

The absolute most toxic town in 'Merica, the name of the riches game in Picher used to be lead and zinc, the mining of which lead to toxicity levels high enough to give one-third of the population lead poisoning. People were evacuated and buildings were demolished due to the shit conditions, and the town was left to sit around in its putrid waste. On top of everything, the shitstorm was stirred up by a massive tornado in 2008. Even with all this, some refused to leave, with only twenty people remaining in 2011. Eventually,

people dumped the dump and the population is now a solid zero. Drinking the water here will get you that much closer to sure death.

RUSH, ARKANSAS

While Arkansas is filled with impressive ghost towns, Rush is the coolest because its original buildings are pretty much intact. People came here looking for silver, but could only dig up zinc. It turns out that the price of zinc stinks, and the town was abandoned in the 1920s. You're allowed to walk around and breathe in the air of abandonment, but stay the fuck away from the mines unless you want to leave Arkansas sans legs.

LAKE SHAWNEE AMUSEMENT PARK, PRINCETON, WEST VIRGINIA

This shit's spooky by even the most critical standards. You don't have to look too hard for ghosts in this amusement park; they're already watching you from the rickety swing set and the eerie Ferris wheel. Not only were a handful of kids killed by freak accidents at this park when it was in operation, but the whole damn thing is built on top of the burial site of thirteen angry Native Americans. We dare you to pretend the creaks and muffled movements are just your imagination.

LOST COVE SETTLEMENT, BORDER OF NORTH CAROLINA AND TENNESSEE

All the moonshine-loving drunks came here during Prohibition because it's out in the woods and away from government eyes. The top population was around one hundred, but when coal replaced timber, the town couldn't quite survive off the grid. This place hasn't seen a soul since 1957 and the cemetery is full of old graves with hand-carved headstones.

HENRY RIVER MILL VILLAGE, HICKORY, NORTH CAROLINA

A boomtown sprang up along the river to pan for gold (and to grow yams?), but as machines replaced people, the town became more and more obsolete. People loved the place but knew they had to leave if they wanted to be gainfully employed, and not just as glorified yam farmers. People held on for as long as they could, and the last person threw in the towel in 1987. The town was ghostly until *The Hunger Games* used it as background and breathed some tourist life into the place.

DEEP IN THE GRAND CANYON

You've seen it in pictures—an orange-to-yellow gradient watercolor that defies reality. But to truly understand the scale of the Grand Canyon in Arizona, employing your 3-D human vision is a must. When you step up to the canyon's edge, you immediately get a sense of how tiny you are. Your stomach will churn and the last thing you'll want to do is descend to the bottom of this giant hole.

But once you've successfully fought off the queasies and told vertigo to suck it, hiking down into the canyon's large crevasses and calling it your cradle for the night is the most exciting way to experience one of America's largest landmarks. It's nippy down there, so bring cover.

HIKING 411

"There are no easy hikes into or out of the Grand Canyon," says the National Park Service, and you know what? It wouldn't be as rewarding if it were easy. A serious warning is to be heeded here: Do not plan to hike from rim to river in one day—250 people are rescued from the canyon each year for being dumb enough to try. You'll need a permit and some knowledge of the length and difficulty of the trail you choose

to hike. Essentials to pack are water, salty snacks, a flashlight, a first aid kit, sunscreen, a hat, a spray bottle filled with water (to keep yourself moist), and a rain jacket (flash summer storms be damned!).

SOUTH RIM

This section gets the most tourist foot traffic, but is still a fun time. The toughest trail here is the Grandview Trail, a steep, rocky monster that's not very long (six

miles round-trip), but will kick your ass anyway. There is no water along the way and boots are a must. In return for your fancy footwork, you get to experience the inner depth of the canyon by way of the Coconino Saddle, and then to the harder-to-hike-to Horseshoe Mesa, where you'll find remnants of (radioactive) copper, the reason behind the creation of this trail in the first place.

OTP Tip: To stay the night, do a round-trip hike and snag one of the three hundred spots at Mather Campground, a civilized resting spot in the village that's open year-round.

NORTH RIM

The hiking equivalent of a bartender's favorite bar to hit after work, the North Rim is where the rangers get their kicks. To do just the tip, Cape Final is an easy four-mile hike that'll have you back in the parking lot in two hours, and offers panoramic views of the canyon from inside. The Tuweep hiking trails are another great undertaking; wherever you start, point your feet toward the Toroweap Overlook, an intense face-to-face meeting with the Colorado River from three thousand vertical feet of solid canyon cliff. If you're the cheatin' kind and want the good views without the exercise, take a jeep to Point Sublime, which pays up on the promises it makes with its name by offering sweeping views of the canyon from east to west.

OTP Tip: At the western section of the Grand Canyon, you'll find brilliant waterfalls that'll make you feel like all that LSD just seeped out of your spine at once. Been there, done that? Try Utah's Bryce Canyon, which comes with the same vertigo but a different rock arrangement.

THE OREGON TRAIL

Get yourself on the Oregon Trail, no ox or covered wagon required this time. The state is more than artisanal doughnuts, birds on bags, and denim shorts. Oregon's abundance of natural wonders will make your craft beer froth over.

THE COAST

Oregon's shoreline is nothing like the overpopulated beaches of the Southern Pacific coastline; in Oregon, all 363 miles of coastline are a wondrous sight. It morphs from cliffs to hidden waterfalls, sand dunes to skate parks, with many points of interest. Haystack Rock is a huge monolith in the ocean, accessible by foot during low tide, where sea creatures cling until the water comes back up. You can find great surfing spots or just choose to get hit in the face with coastal waves that break on the rocks. Either way, the Oregon coast is pretty fucking spectacular.

MOUNT HOOD

Mount Hood offers high-octane hiking, mountain biking, skiing, and summit views you'll need to work hard for to earn. Snow will be up there, in one form or another, as Mount Hood is home to twelve named glaciers. There are six ski areas, and Timberline is the only lift open year-round in all of 'Merica. Standing a proud eleven thousand feet aboveground, this dormant volcano is the tallest mountain in Oregon.

COLUMBIA RIVER GORGE

Who doesn't love a great gorge? This vast gorge is on the Columbia River and is home to the kind of waterfalls under which all your Facebook friends get engaged. This is where you'll roll up your pants, find a walking stick, and wade down the river like a true pioneer. But it's not all wilderness out here; its proximity to Portland washes up all the sour beer, wine, fussy coffee, and baked goods you need to restore your artisanal spirits in Hood River (if Portland had a mini-me city, it'd be this one).

OTP Tip: Hit up the Bonneville Dam in the area, where you can say hi to Herman the Sturgeon, a giant, old fish that swims around in his own exhibit.

THE WALLOWAS

These lowlands will put some real-life scenery behind what you imagined the

Oregon Trail to be in elementary school, complete with ranches, ghost towns, and run-down wagons. Various trails running through the Wallowas can be explored on foot, by bike, on horseback, or in a gondola that'll drop you off at the top of Mount Howard. From there you can see Hells Canyon, 'Merica's deepest canyon at 7,993 feet (which makes the Grand Canyon's 6,000 feet look like a crack in the ground).

PAINTED HILLS

Like a layer cake made of stone, the Painted Hills look as if an artist washed her brushes out into the open hills, with streaks of red and yellow painted on the rocks. Here, you'll find fossils and coyotes. See it several times, because when the sun changes positions, so do the views. The Painted Hills are one part of the John Day Fossil Beds, and if you really need to get some dirt under your nails, head over to Fossil, a nearby town where for $5 you can dig for saber-toothed tigers behind the high school.

SMITH ROCK

The kind of climb that'll break your ankles if you're not careful, Smith Rock is Mother Nature's premier rock-climbing gym, with a few mountain lions and rattlesnakes thrown in to test your courage. Getting to the rock is as awesome as climbing it. Many scenic bikeways wind around it, and you can crawl through a lava tube at Lava River Cave. The city of Bend is twenty-six miles away, and while it's no Portland, you'll still find seventeen breweries and bodacious bites. Take on the rock as many times as you can handle it and high-five a bald eagle at the top.

CRATER LAKE

A 1,946-foot-deep, bright-blue water hole, this crater will make you feel like you're on another planet. The water inside the volcanically created crater is so blue it looks like

an acrylic paint spill. The lake itself is the deepest in 'Merica and going for a swim on most days will freeze your balls right off. The rim of the crater is great to circle by bike, especially at the end of September when the road is closed to other vehicles.

THE FIVE BEST PLACES TO SET UP CAMP

The great outdoors of the West is a nice foil to the traffic-jammed metropolitan cities lining the coast. Plus, plopping down your shit on the ground is a lot cheaper than checking into any hotel. The West's varied landscape means you never have to wake up to the same scenery twice. These are the best red rocks, oceanfront property, and moist grasslands to call home for the night.

BIG SUR, CALIFORNIA

With a sprawling coastline covered in thick vegetation, cliffs, and a few waterfalls that empty directly into the Pacific, setting up camp alongside the 101 Freeway never tasted so good. Just about every car commercial is filmed along this stretch of highway in Northern California, and when the headlights dim, the pollution-free scenery is spectacular. Pitching a tent here after a drive through what seems like a displaced piece of Irish countryside is a relaxing retreat that comes complete with the morning hike of your dreams.

MOUNT SAINT HELENS APE CAVES, WASHINGTON

The camping here is reserved for those who like to scare themselves shitless before bedtime. Ever since Mount Saint Helens, an active volcano, blew her load hard in the '80s, visitors to surrounding Gifford Pinchot National Forest have treaded lightly. While you can't quite spoon the volcano, you can camp at several sites nearby.

Even though it's crowded during peak season, Beaver Bay Campground is particularly good, as it gives you access to a little beach, and puts you in close proximity to the ape caves—several hikable tube caves created by two-thousand-year-old lava deposits. What's the ape part all about? Well, Bigfoot is rumored to roam these parts. Nighttime at the campground gets dark and spooky, and if you hear the ground gurgle, you'd better hope that you'll look good fossilized.

OTP Tip: For a little added kick in the pants, there's a wobbly suspension bridge at Lava Canyon nearby.

CARLSBAD CAVERNS, NEW MEXICO

Limestone lovers, unite! Above the surface the land is unremarkable, but once you hop on the elevator to descend into the depths of the caverns, it turns into a surreal wonderland filled with wacky rock formations, underground lakes, and extra-creepy

noises. The spiky chambers of the Carlsbad Caverns are the perfect place to live out your Batman fantasies, sometimes with real bats.

Close to 800,000 bats are estimated to live in the cave entrance, and, if you time it right, you can see them swirl out of the cave like a tightly wound tornado of furry, flapping bodies. You can't set up camp inside the caverns, but pitching a tent in the backcountry (permit required) puts you within eyeshot of this Indiana Jones–approved underground fantasy world.

OTP Tip: Visit during National Park Week in mid-April when admission to the park is free.

GARDEN OF GODS, COLORADO

While the campgrounds here are less grungy (minus the full-grunge Crags Campground nearby) and more family-oriented, staying amid Colorado's famous red rock formations is worth dealing with the occasional late-night toddler screams. Plus, it puts you within reach of Pikes Peak, the highest point in the Rockies. Hiking to the summit will take some skill and not everybody makes it to the top without succumbing to altitude sickness, but if you've got the chops, the views are incredible. Even from the ground level, you'll discover the "color" of the 'Ado, when the spires of rock gleam in the orange sun, surrounded by green vegetation set against a bright blue sky.

OTP Tip: Check out the insane colors of Maroon Bells right outside of Aspen.

DEATH VALLEY, CALIFORNIA

Try your hand at not dying in Death Valley, the hottest, most dangerous desert in the country. Furnace Creek Campground sits 196 feet below sea level and has tables,

fireplaces, and, most important, toilets. Along with more established hiking routes, the valley has hundreds of miles of backcountry roads (more than any other national park) to explore in a vehicle, or acres of wilderness to navigate on foot. The most important thing here is water. While you won't need to know how to turn your pee into something potable, you will need to stay hydrated, or the vultures (or rattlesnakes, scorpions, and black widows) will circle.

OTP Tip: Death Valley is also home to Badwater Basin, the lowest point in the United States at 282 feet below sea level. Bring your own good water if you want to survive.

GOOGIE GOOD

We don't know about you, but something about the pointed wings and bright colors of the iconic '50s architecture of the WELCOME TO LAS VEGAS sign, worn dull by time, pulls at our heartstrings. Maybe it's the idealization of a period we never got to experience or the comfort of knowing that every establishment with these architectural features will serve us a giant stack of warm pancakes. It all conjures up for us the feeling of simpler times. Whatever it is, this style is iconic in the West and is sadly disappearing.

WILD STYLE

Born in Southern California, this wild style was inspired and driven by the futuristic aesthetic of the jet, space, and atomic ages. The "Googie" style was developed by architect John Lautner in the 1940s and involved flamboyant shapes like boomerangs, parabolas, and flying saucers, plus neon lights, accented by chrome. The swooping, upward-sloping roof and atomic-burst details were captivating to a space travel–obsessed American public, and many diners, motels, and gas stations were built to grab the attention of motorists from the side of the road. The style spread because of its eye-catching qualities as the sprawl of the American population expanded beyond town centers, and people started driving long distances as a pastime. This future-but-retro style got its name from the popular, now-defunct, West Hollywood coffee shop called "Googies."

FUTURE OF RETRO

After the '60s, people fancied themselves more "modern" than Googie. The designs started to look silly and dated, so people actively destroyed Googie structures, determined to wipe out the gaudiness and start fresh. Many incredible structures were destroyed until people changed their minds and started preserving the buildings in the 1990s. All this flip-flopping led to the demolition of some of the coolest structures to grace the West and the development of the concept of "retrofuturism," or the overlap of both looking at the future from the past and looking at the past from the future.

NOTABLE GOOGIES

Bob's Big Boy

A chubby, creepily happy toddler with a burger on a plate is the recognizable mascot of Bob's Big Boy restaurant. Architect Wayne McAllister created the first Big Boy's restaurant, which still stands in Burbank, California. He was inspired by tail fins, apparently loved dingy mustard yellows, and is credited with creating the circular drive-in where carhops would bring diners food on foot or on roller skates.

Big Boy's puts on weekend car shows and occasionally offers carhop service as a throwback to its heyday.

=== *Fun Fact* ===

In 1937, Bob Wian created the "Big Boy," a double-decker that is made up of two patties and a bun sliced in three. The "Big Mac" made its debut in 1967 and McDonald's acquired Big Boy's in 1993.

can be seen from every point on the five roads that converge on this Whittier mainstay. While many car washes were Googied up in the '50s and '60s, this one is the best preserved, perhaps due to its heavy traffic and obnoxiously noticeable neon signage.

NORMS

NORMS isn't as flashy as some Googie-style diners, but it has charm and will not go down without a fight. The quirky structure, with pointy panels all over its roof and sign, first arrived on La Cienega Boulevard in West Hollywood in 1957. NORMS was sold in 2014 after a sixty-five-year run with the Roybark family. It has survived demolition several times and continues to thrive under the shadow of the wrecking ball.

Oldest (Operating) McDonald's

This building's facade has been attracting gluttonous motorists since 1953 and is a step into a simpler time, when a burger was just a burger and a heart attack was something that happened to unicorns. This particular Micky Dee's, complete with rolling golden arches lined with neon, was built in Downey, a suburb of LA with booming aerospace companies. While many goofy Googie McDonald's were destroyed around the country, this one stood its ground and was named a historic landmark in 1983.

Johnie's

First opened in 1956, this empty, closed Miracle Mile diner eerily still feels as if it has a little life left in it. The blue-and-white-striped, sloped roof displays dingy red signs and oddly, without a single customer inside, still lights up at night. Johnie's is owned by the guy behind the 99 Cents Only Store and only opens the shop for the entertainment industry. Johnie's appeared in *Reservoir Dogs*, *American History X*, and *The Big Lebowski*.

Five Points Car Wash

Built in 1963, this car wash has a roof with distinctive towering, angular features that

=== *Fun Fact* ===

The first-ever McDonald's was in Des Plaines, Illinois. It was turned into a museum with mannequins instead of servers, and creepily stands, shuttered, across the street from a modern McCafé.

THE FIVE BEST DINERS IN 'MERICA

Fancy feasts be damned! Sometimes the only way to feed your deepest cravings is at a greasy spoon, where the waitresses have that huggable quality, the portions are stupid-big, and every bite tastes like a piece of 'Merica. From spinning stools to quarter per play jukeboxes, slouch down in these five best diners around the country.

THE SOUTH

Brent's Drugs, Jackson, Mississippi

All the diner flair with cheese oozing out of every burger and perfectly cooked eggs any way you take 'em, but with the added benefit of a hidden speakeasy cocktail bar.

THE YANKEES

The Blue Benn Diner, Bennington, Vermont

There are jukeboxes on every wall (and at the counter), swivel stools and booths, laminated "specials" attached to every overhead place imaginable, and a hefty menu of favorites like eggs Benedict, pancakes, and slices of pie the size of your face.

MIDDLE 'MERICA

Al's Breakfast, Minneapolis, Minnesota

In the heart of Dinkytown, Al's is a little Euro diner where people clamor to get their asses in one of the fourteen available seats. Al's serves updated classics under twinkly lights. A blueberry pancake here will span your entire plate and come with a pat of melting butter.

NEBRASKA AND THE LIKE

Franks Diner, Kenosha, Wisconsin

This place has been tellin' it like it is since 1921, when the diner was a train car dragged into town from New Jersey to feed the hungry citizens. The special here is called a "garbage plate," a wonderful mess of five eggs, hash browns, and meats of your choosing.

THE GODDAMN HIPPIES

Bette's Oceanview Diner, Berkeley, California

This place has only been around since 1982, but serves seriously killer soufflé pancakes, and corned beef hash, and can poach an egg like nobody's business. While it doesn't come with an ocean view, it does have an artistic slice of pie hanging from the ceiling.

NAVAJO SILVERSMITHING

All around the high desert of the Southwest, especially in Arizona, you'll find one-of-a-kind jewelry crafted from gorgeous silver and studded with precious minerals and stones. This isn't some trinket shit you'll get at a mall; these pieces are unique to the region and made by some knowledgeable hands.

NAVAJO NATION

A semiautonomous region that dips into Northeast Arizona, Southeast Utah, and Northwest New Mexico, the Navajo Nation is a thriving Native American community. But that wasn't always the case. The Long Walk (from 1864 to 1866) was a forced deportation by foot of the Navajo people from their reservation in Arizona to an internment camp called Bosque Redondo in New Mexico to make room for white settlers.

After a lot of serious bullshit and miraculous negotiation on the part of the Navajo, they were granted reservation land and had to take the long walk back home to what is now termed "Navajo Nation." The reservation is set against the backdrop of Navajo Mountain, which was always regarded as a symbol of great cultural importance. To this day, climbing the mountain is prohibited.

TURQUOISE

Before European contact, the Navajo mined for turquoise in Mineral Park, a mine filled with the stuff, near Kingman, Arizona. Traditionally, the Navajo believe turquoise brings luck, health, and happiness, and is used to ward off negativity and raise self-confidence. The bright stone accents Navajo-made heishi necklaces, or strings of perfectly whittled beads created from shells, minerals, and stones, crafted as symbols of artistry and to be used ceremoniously.

When turquoise contains more copper, the color is blue; if it's found near zinc, the color is more yellow. Iron gives it a greenish hue, while aluminum makes it white. Since it is formed using the metals that surround it, turquoise varies greatly from region to region, and, for the Navajo, acts as a visual connection to the land where it's from.

SILVER

The Navajo didn't work with silver until the introduction of silversmithing by traders in the nineteenth century. One man, Atsidi Sani, started to cast silver in sandstone and pound it out with a hammer. By 1880, he had taught his craft to his sons, and others soon began creating jewelry by pounding out U.S. coins. When that became illegal, they used Mexican pesos. These artisans combined silver with local turquoise to create what we now call Navajo jewelry. Different tribes, like the Hopi and the Zuni, also learned the craft and began developing their own designs. At first, the Navajo made jewelry only for themselves and other Native Americans. Then the opening of the transcontinental railroad in 1869 brought an influx of people who wanted their jewelry as adornments, without any higher purpose.

METAL MEETS STONE COLD STEALING

Between 1892 and 1899, Tiffany & Company extracted $2 million worth of turquoise from the Cerrillos area in New Mexico. In 1900, Tiffany's presented a collection of "Native American–inspired" designs at the Paris World's Fair, which won the company many awards and led to Tiffany's appointment as the official jewelers for royalty in Europe, the Ottoman Empire, and Russia.

JUXTAPOSED DWELLINGS: ART IN VENICE, CALIFORNIA

Venice is the most expensive slum anywhere. Million-dollar houses stand beside homeless lean-tos, and the ocean is everyone's backyard. Imagine a section of coastline where every skater, old punk, hippie, and fly-by-night swindler converged and set up shop. People traveling westward make Venice their final destination, and some of the nuttiest people decide to stay. With this many creative (and crazy) minds in one place, some interesting visual shit's bound to happen. This is the art that comes from the poster city of economic disparity.

CLOWNERINA

A thirty-foot-tall, dolled-up man clown with a five o'clock shadow and wearing a tutu hangs over the CVS on Main Street as a big ol' terrifying welcome sign to Venice. What the hell's it doing up there? Originally built in 1988 by Jonathan Borofsky as an art piece for a museum, Clownerina exemplifies Venice's contradictions. Part street performer, part classical dancer, Clownerina is one of the most photographed installations in the city.

═══ Fun Fact ═══

The clown's leg is mechanized and is built to kick, but after a year of loud squeaking noises, the neighbors had his leg shut off. In 2014, the clown's leg got lubed and now kicks into action from 1 to 6 p.m. every day.

GRAFFITI WALL

A stretch of concrete in the middle of the beach, this wall has a heartwarming history. It used to be part of the Venice Pavilion and people sprayed it up with colorful murals. When that building was torn down, the walls were preserved because the community couldn't part with the art. In 2000,

the wall became a legal graffiti space, and today, artists work with In Creative Unity (a graffiti production company) to paint it while the ocean rolls around nearby.

JIM MORRISON

In an alley just a few steps up from the boardwalk, you'll meet the vacant stare and shirtless body of Jim Morrison, on the side of an apartment building, painted by Rip Cronk in 1991. During the '60s, the Doors spent a lot of time living like gypsies and recording in Venice. This portrait puts you in the acid-trippin', canal-hopping, beach-sleeping mood that inspired the psychedelic tunes of one of America's greatest bands.

STREET VENDORS

You'll see what makes Venice special sprawled out all over the boardwalk. From makeshift henna studios to sand art, twisted metal sculptures to paintings of wolves howling across rainbow landscapes, artists on the boardwalk offer for sale every

colorful, quirky thing you can imagine. In addition to art, this stretch of oceanside concrete is teeming with buskers of all persuasions, sometimes on rollerblades.

FANCY GALLERIES

Like a page out of *Juxtapoz* magazine, Abbot Kinney is a street full of fancy galleries and the kind of people who like to peruse them. Standing in stark contrast to the rest of Venice, but somehow still an integral part of this vibrant city, the tree-lined blocks here are filled with dreamy lofts and high-stakes art.

C.A.V.E. Gallery always has the kind of art on display that you're afraid to get near, the kind of stuff that's so clean and neat that you check your fingernails to make sure there isn't grime lingering underneath. In the snazzy G2 building, you'll find intricate exhibits that you stop and admire at a distance. Nearby, the restaurant scene is all small plates and big rents. This, too, is Venice, flipped on its head and scrubbed of all its dirty parts.

HIPPIE HAUTE

A look that developed in the '60s in response to the tensions of the Vietnam War, hippie fashion (or lack thereof) grew out of the black on black of the Beatniks, but added a flower power, peace, and love aesthetic. Achieving that loose and free look is easy, but you'll need to make some fashion compromises.

While the real era of the hippie is long gone, much of the West, especially San Francisco, still sports a version of that smelly, sexy, styleless style. First and foremost, you'll need to get high. The choice of drug is yours, but make sure you see colors. Now let's get you sloppily dressed, you dirty hippie.

FABRIC OF OUR LIVES

This style is all about getting back to nature, and breaking ties with The Man, industrialization, and technology. This means that what you're wearing is either really loose or you're naked. Cotton, linen, and hippie hemp are the preferred fabrics, and prints that have been around since the '60s are safe bets. If you can work tie-dye or purple into your ensemble, you're on the right track. Underwear is optional. Bras? Nah.

CRUSTY TOES AREN'T A NO-NO

The hippie movement is all about freedom from the white picket fence, and that sort of freedom is best achieved by not wearing shoes. Okay, sometimes sandals, but grooming your feet is a nothing if you're really doing it the hippie way. You feel the Earth with your feet, which means you sometimes step on a hypodermic needle or a pile of vomit. But that's feet freedom, friends.

CRYSTAL POWER

Jewels and gems are used as tripping tools, so the more wacky, prismlike the designs, the better. If you can work a crystal into a ring or as a pendant, you will be praised by the powers that be. Believe it or not, peace-sign earrings are still popular in hippie hot spots like Sedona, Arizona, and Northern California.

OTP Tip: Learn to weave a flower wreath. It'll be the coolest accessory in all the land, until it rots and dies.

CARPET HAIR

Whether we're talking about your face, legs, pits, or head, hair is left to grow to its longest length. As one of the most notable hippie habits, stylish haircuts do not exist in hippieland. This is how white people dreads happen. It's not pretty.

SMELL BAD, IT'S GOOD

If you're really going to commit to this hippie thing, we'll need you to put your deodorant into the recycling bin right now. To replace the oppressing, store-bought potion, grab a bunch of sage. Light it, wave it around, and now you smell the way you should.

UFO MANIA!

If you want to get in on the mania surrounding the possible existence of alien life, Roswell, New Mexico, will hook you up. The town has been obsessed with UFOs for decades. Roswell is littered with UFO-related memorabilia and populated by conspiracy theorists of all stripes.

It all started in 1947 when a rancher reported strange debris he found in a field to the Air Force. Despite reassurance from the military that the junk was not from outer space, people were hooked on the idea of alien contact. Since then, Roswellians have been diggin' for the scoop on flying saucers, claiming sightings of outer space light formations and creating a culture around UFOs. There's a UFO museum, a kooky UFO Festival, and more serious conferences that attempt to uncover what the fuck is really going on.

=== *Fun Fact* ===

While Nevada's Area 51 is said to be the site of alien activity, it's an operating military airfield, and, well, sometimes shit is launched from there into the air. People are so convinced that the whole place is a cover-up for alien life that the road leading up to it is called "Extraterrestrial Highway," and there's even a place called Little A'Le'Inn, where you can eat, sleep, and buy an array of alien merch.

HOW TO LOOK THE PART IN LA

Even if you don't aspire to be the best background extra in the industry, Hollywood has a hold on Los Angeles and its style sensibility. People go outside to be seen, and hide in their cars when they're not at their best. When locals aren't wearing yoga pants (and some people still are), this is how to look the part in different parts of LA.

WEST HOLLYWOOD

West Hollywood is the intersection of gay culture, Russians, tourists, coffee shop-dwelling screenwriters, Russians, and club kids making their first discovery that a skirt can more effectively be worn as a dress. The style here is as eclectic as the area's residents, but do count on fanny packers, flip-flopped coffee shops, and "hiking" apparel with a full face of makeup strolling around Runyon Canyon during the day. The nighttime brings "fast fashion," in all its glittery glory, and shitty quality made in faraway lands (likely Koreatown in Downtown LA) and distributed along Melrose Avenue. West Hollywood musts: a tan and a strong core. Clothes go somewhere on top of that.

SANTA MONICA

In Santa Monica, when the weather dips below 70, you'd better have your Uggs ready, because it's winter and everyone will be bitching about how freezing it is. Sure, it gets a bit breezy by the beach, but the yoga moms run for cover in their $100 white T-shirts at the sight of a cloud. The rule about LA's beaches is the farther south you go into Manhattan, Redondo, and Orange County, the more expensive the beach attire gets and the more Republican the politics become.

"GREATER" LOS ANGELES

Nobody gives a shit about fashion once you get out of the LA city limits. To be stylish here, what you do is pick an LA sports team and deck out your car, baby, and person in said team's merch. Places like Downey, West Covina, and Whittier mostly wear Dodgers jerseys, with an occasional Lakers fan who still defends the honor of the Shaq and Kobe power duo days.

SILVERLAKE

Dig into your grandpa's suspenders drawer, because things are about to get hipster. While this area (along with Eagle Rock, Larchmont, and Echo Park) was no man's land for the longest time, it has become a mecca of everything fashionably irreverent. If you find yourself in Silverlake on a Saturday morning, put on something that says, "I am going to spend all afternoon drinking cold brew at Intelligentsia and browsing vintage records, then go gastro-pub-hopping with other Angeleno-by-way-of-Milwaukee transplants."

DOWNTOWN

As long as you've got pockets, and those pockets are filled with cash, whatever you're wearing is acceptable—unless you have a beater car. Then park it far away or underground.

THE VALLEY

The Valley, specifically Van Nuys, is where the porn of America is made. Take that as you will, but when it comes to fashion, sometimes shit gets slutty. You'll be at the supermarket and fishnets will hit your periph in the produce section more

often than not. You can participate in the pasty party to fit in, or opt for something more wholesome. The Valley is always ten degrees hotter than the rest of LA, so those booty shorts may be your only option in the summer.

FOOD

IF YOU CAN'T GET IT IN PORTLAND, IT DOESN'T EXIST

Portland is a place that's so ridiculously artisanal that it has a sarcastic TV show that, season after season, comes up with funny new ways to talk about this dynamic city. Whatever you're craving, Portland's got a number of places that'll hit the spot. Don't forget to put a bird on it.

SALTY

Just saying *charcuterie* out loud makes you more artisanal than the general population, and in Portland you take your small talk up a step by hitting Olympic Provisions for something salty. Depending on the day, your board may be loaded with sopressata, chorizo, saucisson, mortadella, salami, or head cheese terrine. Hit Pok Pok for fish sauce–doused chicken wings, pig out on the whole pig plate at Higgins, and chow the world-famous porchetta sandwich at Lardo to give your salty cravings something to write home about.

SWEET

While Voodoo Doughnuts isn't the best sweet, fried dough you can get around here, it's the most popular. Lines are always inexplicably out the door and the maple bacon bar is likely what their sweet teeth

are all waiting around for. Unless they're in line for the cock-and-balls, a huge, cream-in-the-right-places doughnut you'll need to make room for in your pants.

OTP Tip: For colder sweets, check out Portland's ice cream palace Salt & Straw. With flavors like Pear and Blue Cheese, Honey Balsamic and Black Pepper, and seasonal vegetable concoctions, Salt & Straw's level of creativity will satisfy you on multiple levels.

SOUR

Can you pickle this? In Portland, the answer is always an emphatic *hell yes*! Sure, this town has specialty stores (with cutesy names like MoonBrine) that sell jars of the stuff, but if you were ever in the mood to get wacky with your cravings, this is the place.

Killer Burger is a mini-chain with a Peanut Butter Pickle Bacon Burger on the menu, which will make that baby in your belly kick even if you're nowhere near pregnant. Just about any bar will hook you up with a pickle plate filled with an assortment of veggies. (Check out the Old Gold plate of pickled cauliflower, bell pepper, onions, and goddamn pears.)

Fun Fact

People in Portland know everyone makes fun of them. So much so that they decided to go with the humble pickle as a mascot for an amateur baseball team . . . because they can pickle that.

BITTER

When it comes to curing your craving for all things with bitter bite, Portland's got two sippable solutions: beer and coffee. With the 216 craft breweries (that's 7.4 beer places per capita) in Oregon, it's estimated that 53 percent of beer made here is consumed by its residents. You can't go wrong with a flight from Deschutes Brewery or Bailey's Taproom, and a Sweet Heat pint at Fire on the Mountain, made with apricot purée and Scotch bonnet chilis, which will nip that bitter craving in the bud, with a few stops along the flavor rainbow.

When it comes to coffee, Portland is on its third wave (while the rest of the country tries to figure out how to surf the first). That means they've moved on from just making and selling the bean to super-specializing it to suit artisanal palates. A frothy latte from fussy places like Coava Coffee Roasters and Barista will wake you up from your bitter beer slump and make you feel like king of the bean.

OTP Tip: Follow this up with a flaming Spanish coffee from Huber's to combine the bitters of both coffee and booze with a kick of fire.

DO-GOODER

If your cravings are for good feelings in addition to tasty bites, there are options in Portland to handle that. Hit Brass Tacks for housemade vegan meat sandwiches (with pickles and tomato jam), Sizzle Pie for a vegan slice, and Food Fight! (an all-vegan grocery store) for whatever odds and ends you need to leave the city feeling like you haven't harmed a thing. Portland is also home to the world's only vegan strip club, Casa Diablo, which means you can even do good while being naughty.

OTP Tip: At OTP we believe that "cheap" is a reasonable craving, and Portland is America's food cart and truck mecca. So much so that there's a duel (Cartopia versus Cartlandia) between which area has the best set of pods, stands, trucks, and carts.

MEXICAN FOOD MASSACRE

While the United States was founded by a whole bunch of immigrants, 'Merica fights hard to keep its borders sealed from intruders, especially those from Mexico. California's agricultural industry is a big draw for food cultivators, and migrant workers from Mexico have historically brought their food, music, and culture to the places in which they settled for work. There is some mighty Mexican food to be found all along the coast, with the three biggest contenders being San Diego, Los Angeles, and San Francisco. While there is much debate about which one serves up the best, each place has its own deliciously unique take on Mexi-Cali cuisine. Let them fight; we're here to eat.

SAN DIEGO

As the closest big city to the border, San Diego's Mexican is raw and real, except when you feel like eating a nothing-authentic-about-it, nacholike mess atop an ungodly amount of French fries, then one of the 'Berto's has got your back.

Mexican food was first introduced to San Diegans through Roberto's, who lovingly stuffed French fries into a burrito to create the distinctive California Burrito, and many 'Berto spinoffs (like JilBerto's and

Alberto's) have ridden on the tail of Rob's burrito trail since. SD is also home to the best baja fish tacos, filled with crisp fried filets, a crunchy slaw, and a good squeeze of lime. Popping a few on the beach before hitting the waves is the culturally appropriate thing to do year-round. Don't wait thirty minutes to get in the water—fish tacos act as a natural flotation device.

VERSUS LOS ANGELES

Ask any Angelino, and he'll spit in the open face of SD's fish tacos, claiming LA's are far superior. Sometimes Mexican food comes here to get poshed-up, LA style, but the nooks and crannies of this town (i.e., the places that claim to be LA and are given a "Greater LA" title as a pacifier) are where all the authenticity lives. Hitting Ricky's Fish Tacos truck in Silverlake puts your mouth in the front row of shrimp and fish taco heaven, while Coni'Seafood out in Inglewood serves up a marlin taco with some fierce spicy salsa, and El Coraloense down in Downey has the kind of ceviche that'll make you pucker with pure joy.

And it's not just fish in LA, either; many a meat finds its juicy way to a freshly flattened corn tortilla here. But as much as LA will claim its burrito game is quite formidable, nobody can deny that SF is the reigning burrito champ.

OTP Tip: Tito's Tacos in Culver City is a taco stand legend, known for its crunchy tacos, like the kind you get at Taco Bell, but shouldn't.

VERSUS SAN FRANCISCO

While Southern Cali is messin' with tacos, SF stands proud with the burrito game on lock. The Mission super-burrito is undoubtedly the best rolled-up log of Mexican food you'll get in 'Merica. The "super" part is just the addition of sour cream and guac, but these burritos are truly heroic. These monster burritos can be found on just about every block of the 24th Street corridor in the Mission, with El Farolito headlining the burrito-fest on Mission Street. You'll get three-quarters of the way down your silver wrapper and wonder how you'll ever finish. Persevere; the burrito coma awaits.

Most 'Mericans eat what they feel comfortable with. As such, carne asada tacos, quesadillas, and burritos (i.e., the most reminiscent of familiar sandwiches) are the most popular Mexican dishes. But the cuisine is very diverse, and you'll find some crazy-ass shit in tiny carts parked across California (like brains, many a fish head, blood, and stomach-lining soup, stews, and the like). Poke your nose into anything that smells good and get the greasiest thing you see.

SEATTLE SELLS CRACK

Seattle definitely gets real high off its own supply, consuming more coffee than any other city in America. We can't think of a better way to beat the gloom than a hot cup of freshly brewed coffee. Always sit by a big window, because, in Seattle, watching the rain is an actual activity that people do. Here's how coffee got so hot here.

COFFEE HISTORY

Starbucks didn't invent coffee drinking, but it sure did a good job pushing it to the American public as a trendy sip—and it all started in Seattle. In the '70s, Starbucks (named after a character in *Moby-Dick*) was just a shop that sold beans and bean machines. In 1977, it moved to Pike Place and began brewing drinks and creating that love-to-hate butchery of Italian words and elevator music coffee culture.

SBUX wasn't the only one slinging the bean, but it swallowed up competitors like Seattle's Best, later rebranding that as the poor man's Starbucks to push it into new markets. And then there's Tully's, a company that opened its first shop in 1992

with the aim of directly competing with SBUX. Playing with fire got Tully's beans burnt and it filed for bankruptcy in 2012.

THE ESPRESSO AGE (AKA PISSING OFF ITALIANS)

While Starbucks focused on growing into a megacorp beast, local coffee lovers drew their attention to coddling, cupping, refining, and making sweet latte love to the coffee bean. Push-button extraction was replaced by people who gave a genuine fuck about the final product, and places like Victrola, Espresso Vivace, and Caffe Vita thrived, serving specialty coffee and pulling consistently creamy shots for weather-worn Seattleites.

The local bean game exploded, with Seattle roasters taking top accolades across all of America, and the concentration of shops (2.5 per 100,000 residents in 2012) grew to ten times more than anywhere else in the country.

In every gloomy nook of Seattle, you will find superb coffee and fierce baristas preparing it for you, using whatever method you prefer. People in this city describe coffee with wine terms and they drink it like water. Bouncing from one café to the next is an experience unique to Seattle, with each offering something special, like its own rain-viewing window, vitamin D lamp (that's a thing, believe it or not), or that special worn-in grandpa chair. There are also coffee drive-throughs and many places deliver. But how do you set yourself apart from the single-origin herd?

DIFFERENTIATION

When you've micro-brewed, super-sourced, and overfussed your coffee to the max, you have to do something really special to get customers to choose your cup over the millions of others in town. One approach is to impress people with impeccable latte art; combine your coffee with cupcakes, flowers, and the post office; or get your baristas to wear bikinis and lick whipped cream off each other.

Bikini baristas are filthy unicorns only found in Washington state. While you won't find them in downtown Seattle, the outskirts of the city are dotted with shacks run by ladies in bikinis, crappily pulling shots because they're trying to avoid getting espresso grounds into delicate places. Is it slightly trailer park-ish? Why, yes, it is. But when just a smile with your coffee won't do, hit up Cowgirls Espresso for a possible nip slip latte.

THE SUSHI BOOM

It's almost inconceivable that Americans would ever acquire a taste for raw fish. There had to be a lot of handholding at the fishy beginning, right? Sushi started as Japanese street food until the 1800s, when refrigeration came along and changed the game. Fish began swimming around the world postmortem, with a version of sushi slowly wiggling onto American plates and eventually setting off a tidal wave of raw enthusiasm.

RAW FISH FOR THE MICROWAVE DINNER CROWD?

Imagine convincing true blue 'Mericans in the '50s that that mush they call tuna in their casserole should be eaten raw. And not just raw fish, but try telling someone who's been putting ketchup on everything that what they should be doing is dipping this raw fish into something green and spicy as fuck. Then chasing it with a pickled root.

A lot of times, cultural conflicts result in not just aggression but an exchange of food. We all have to eat, and soldiers fighting overseas during World War II were no different. That's why it's not surprising that when they came back, sushi picked up speed in the '50s around San Diego, known for its military bases. A place called Miyako first served sushi and sashimi, but mingled the menu with Cantonese dishes, lots of cooked items, and Hawaiian spare ribs in a kitschy Japanese atmosphere, complete with kimono-ed waitresses.

═══ Fun Fact ═══

Tuna in Japan was cat food in the '50s. Nuclear tests in the Pacific caused a shortage of tuna, so the Japanese government began marketing it as a delicacy in response to the higher prices brought on by (low) supply and (high) demand.

AMERICANIZED BITS

At the beginning of the sushi craze, people couldn't distinguish between Japanese cuisine and the food of other Asian countries. So places would serve all kinds of dishes—Chinese to Thai—under the Japanese name, because it carried an exoticism and cachet that allowed owners to charge more. And this wasn't traditional Japanese fare; this was food finagled to fit the sweet- and fat-loving American palate.

WTF is a California Roll?

The California roll is like sushi with training wheels, using familiar ingredients rolled in seaweed. Imitation crab (surimi) was invented in Japan, but America produces a shit ton of it. It was used to both circumvent overfishing of bluefin tuna (otoro) and to push sushi to more Americans in forms they could handle. California rolls broke sushi from the tradition of simplicity, and America built on the idea by shoving all kinds of things into rolls. Cream cheese and fish? Sure you don't just want it on a bagel?

Japanese food entered America by sweetening its meats. While teriyaki did originate in Japan, the idea of making it cloyingly sweet and adding sesame seeds and garlic is all-American. This dish reminded Americans of BBQ and we got fully behind it. Edamame was also an easy sell, as it was introduced with beer and could be eaten in place of peanuts.

Eventually, as people grew accustomed to the idea of sushi, more traditional preparations became posh and the trend moved to Hollywood to feed the elite. Sushi jumped coasts, with actors like Robert De Niro pushing Nobu Matsuhisa to open his now world-famous Southern and sushi fusion joint, Nobu, in New York.

SUSHI GOES BOTH WAYS

But the growth of sushi can't just be attributed to America's junky palates. It went both ways. Sushi mastery in Japan is a painstakingly long process; you don't even touch the fish until you've put in six years in a restaurant's kitchen. With the expansion of sushi as an in-demand food around the Pacific Rim, aspiring Japanese chefs left the island and found solace in America. Their culinary penchant to experiment with raw and cooked ingredients was welcomed on our shores; customers and bosses wouldn't criticize their creations if they weren't 100 percent traditional. America became a place where sushi was both bastardized and innovated.

The spike in fish consumption created a new global marketplace around the world's oceans. Fish is caught in New England and sold to Tsukiji Market in Japan, and from there it is resold to top restaurants in LA and NYC. Why? Because we still think that the Japanese know how shit should be done and don't dare butcher a freshly caught tuna ourselves.

=== *Fun Fact* ===

Red tuna against white rice is a symbol of nationalism, and the Japanese love their tuna because it is a fighting fish. It takes four to five hours to wrestle one on the line, sometimes fighting to the death, and a tuna swims as fast as a Porsche 911, accelerating from 0 to 50 in three seconds.

MUSIC

RED ROCKS AMPHITHEATRE

America has spectacular music venues, where many a legend has played. But no space in this great land is as coveted as the Red Rocks Amphitheatre in Morrison, Colorado, for fans and performers alike. Sure, hearing a concert inside an enclosed stadium is fun and great, but what does it sound like when Mother Nature sets up a performance space of her own? The Red Rocks Amphitheatre is a picturesque sculpture of towering rocks with the kind of acoustics that'll make sound engineers squirm in their seats.

HEARING IS BELIEVING

As a musical meeting point between the Great Plains and the Rockies, sounds at the Red Rocks Amphitheatre bounce off Ship Rock and Creation Rock, two giant red sandstone monoliths that are both taller than Niagara Falls (and contain actual dinosaur fossils!). While some of the foundation and seating is human-made, the majority of the space has been created by years of erosion and other geological activity. A show here is better than any football stadium production.

HOW THE ROCKS ROLL

Officially open as a music venue since 1941, Red Rocks was named the top amphitheater in the country by numerous music big shots, including the editors of *Rolling Stone*. The Rocks host every genre, from single singers like Lana del Rey to metalheads like Mastodon, and a summer EDM festival that'll get you trippin' rocks. Among countless others, the Beatles performed here in 1964, the Eagles in 1975, and Paul Oakenfold threw a massive rave here in 2000.

NOT SET IN STONE

While there are some rules to follow come concert night, many are loosely enforced as long as you're not a jerk to nature and clean up after yourself. You're not supposed to bring booze and joints into the venue, but many either tailgate in the parking lots or quietly enjoy their libations inside. Cig smokers: You're SOL.

THE DEETS ON DENVER

Passing out in the middle of the Rocks is not okay, but nearby Denver will cradle your sleepy head. It's only seventeen miles away, and not only are you allowed to legally smoke all the weed you want there, but downtown is now packed with all the coffee, pastries, craft beers, froufrou restaurants, and expertly prepared cocktails you'll ever need. In addition, Denver is known for its breweries and it's too easy to get caught up touring those bad boys and forget you've got a show to catch. Then there's summer skiing.

With a capacity of about ten thousand, a show at Red Rocks is always a memorable experience. Not only is the scenery mind-blowingly beautiful, but the surrounding acres of nature don't care how loud you scream.

SASQUATCH! MUSIC FESTIVAL

The Sasquatch! festival is a one-up on the scary stories you tell at summer camp. A musical celebration in the land of folklore, Sasquatch! doesn't guarantee a Bigfoot sighting, but a good time is definitely guaranteed. You will come to Sasquatch! a regular music reveler, but leave a wild, hairy man, running into the night, leaving only tracks behind.

HOAX HISTORY

You don't need to know anything about Sasquatch to enjoy the festival, but it's a lot more fun to be informed, and maybe get some inspiration for pulling some pranks yourself. Grab your monkey suit and rubber feet, and get ready to piss off some partygoers.

The first alleged sightings can be traced back to Native American populations of the Pacific Northwest, who describe a larger-than-life creature lurking in the night shadows. Interestingly enough, almost every culture has a humanoid giant in its folkloric history, perhaps a manifestation of our universal fascination with the thrill of fear. Sightings in the region date back to the 1850s, with many accounts claiming that a hairy, seven-foot-tall

mountain creature abducted their friends. Some reported full-on Sasquatch families, while others have spotted huge footprints in the forest.

A number of films and photographs have made it into the mainstream media, and while some were confirmed hoaxes (the most famous of which was the 1967 Patterson-Gimlin footage), others are still up in the air. Science quashes the idea of the 'Squatch (and his cousins the Yeti and the Abominable Snowman), but the general public still likes to believe in the lore, especially late at night.

PARTY TIME

Once you're done bigfooting around, you'll notice that the festival takes place in a stunning amphitheater carved out of the basalt cliffs soaring above the Columbia River Gorge in Quincy, Washington. The four-day fest draws in some seriously great acts, like Gogol Bordello, Hot Chip, Tame Impala, and Kendrick Lamar, and is spread across five stages (namely, Twix Yeti, Bigfoot, Sasquatch, Uranus, and El Chupacabra). The pumping music should make you feel primal in no time and stir whatever may lurk in the shadows.

ONE WITH 'SQUATCH

This is a fun festival to camp out around. Since it's in a gorge, you can't quite pop in and pop out. There's a glamping option, but at $2,500 per ticket, we recommend pretending to be Sasquatch from the comforts of your own sleeping bag in the well-equipped campground surrounding the fest. While showers are available around the site for a small fee, if you're really trying to scare the shit out of people, stay stinky, friends. According to people who claim to have had close encounters with the 'Squatch, the creature has a very strong body odor. If you're going for authenticity, make sure you spend enough time dancing to acquire this special stench.

=== *Fun Fact* ===

The only Bigfoot trap in existence, a large wooden box secured to the ground by telephone poles, has been sitting in a remote area of Jackson County, Oregon, since 1974.

THE TEN BEST WESTERN SALOONS

Saloons were places where miners, gamblers, and cowboys went to unwind, pick up a bar lady, and shoot at their friends and enemies for fun. But the saloon had a big bull target on its back from the get-go, they didn't keep regular hours, and served minors (and women). "Temperance forces" (those who lobbied for Prohibition) made sure to bring these infractions to the attention of governing bodies. These ten places won the duel, standing their booze-soaked ground.

GENOA BAR & SALOON, GENOA, NEVADA

The oldest "thirst parlor" in the state of Nevada, the Genoa Bar has been in operation since 1853. The inside smells of rotten scoundrels, with a hint of John Wayne and Clint Eastwood, both of whom have made films here. Gather 'round the wood-burning stove (you'll have no choice during winter because it's the only source of heat in these parts), and take a deep breath to fill your lungs with the dust of the good ol' days (and the grime particles coming off Raquel Welch's decrepit bra, which hangs on the deer-head antlers).

CRYSTAL PALACE SALOON, TOMBSTONE, ARIZONA

The town of Tombstone alone should tell you a lil' somethin' about the area establishments. The Crystal Palace started as a brewery called the Golden Eagle, which was demolished by a fire that swept through Tombstone between 1881 and 1882. It was rebuilt with a goldfish pond in the center that was said to spout fresh water, and morphed first into a fine-dining establishment and then a palace of drunks and gamblers Today, the Crystal Palace is, according to the bar's slogan, "still serving good whiskey and tolerable water," and while the goldfish have long swum upstream to the pond in the sky, kitschy costumed waitresses and bartenders keep the spirit of the West alive.

IRON DOOR SALOON, GROVELAND, CALIFORNIA

While it's debatable whether this saloon is the oldest in California (as touted by its proprietors), it does get the award for the most literal name, as its doors are made of pure, swinging iron. The town's postmaster used to own the saloon, from 1863 to 1880, running his mail business from behind the bar (which likely resulted in the mail equivalent of drunk texts). Located twenty-five miles from the mouth of Yosemite, the Iron Door Saloon is a great place to warm your belly before entering the wilderness.

BUCKHORN EXCHANGE, DENVER, COLORADO

Do you like taxidermied mountain lions, deer, and 'coons? Buck up to the Buckhorn Exchange, where animal eyes ogle you from the walls. Opened in 1893, this place is five minutes from downtown Denver, but a century away from modern times. Buckhorn holds the city's first liquor license and the kitchen serves up buffalo, elk, quail, rattlesnake, and alligator—the kind of stuff that railroaders ate on their downtime.

BUCKET OF BLOOD SALOON, VIRGINIA CITY, NEVADA

This saloon may have been covered in blood buckets back in the day, but its current condition, decked out in Tiffany lamps and mirrors, is a little less sanguine. Built in 1876 after a fire wiped out the whole town in 1875, the Bucket of Blood still retains some old-timey masonry walls with faint remnants of doorways, one of which used to lead to the Boston Saloon, a thriving African-American bar taken out by the flames.

PIONEER SALOON, GOODSPRINGS, NEVADA

The biggest reason to come here is to become a certified asshole. That's right! The Asshole Association was formed here to gather together drunk assholes in the name of charity. They hold an annual toy drive and maintain a daily tarantula-juice-drinkin' habit. The bar itself is wrapped in tin and newspaper clippings from 1916, and once had an attached hotel where laypeople and assholes alike could get comfortable with dancing girls.

EL PATIO CANTINA, MESILLA, NEW MEXICO

Officially established in 1934, this bar has been boozing it up since way before it became official. Originally owned by Billy the Kid's lawyer, El Patio is now a better place to shoot pool than villains, drink cheap beers, and, oddly, listen to rap music blasted at a volume that'll piss you off enough to pistol-whip another patron.

1880 UNION HOTEL, LOS ALAMOS, CALIFORNIA

An in-between rest stop for tired nine-teenth-century railroaders traveling be-tween San Francisco and Los Angeles, or those taking the stagecoach, this hotel has been comforting weary travelers since—you guessed it—1880. While the entire place is decked out in Victorian decor, the attached saloon's spirit is up on the times. Paul McCartney, Michael Jackson, and Jon Bon Jovi have filmed music videos here, and Johnny Cash used to bring his guitar by to play live on the regular circuit back in the '50s.

POZO SALOON, SANTA MARGARITA, CALIFORNIA

A San Luis Obispo landmark since 1858, the Pozo Saloon is also a beefy restaurant and music venue. It's a perfect mix of old timey saloon with a bar that's all about the 1800s and an outdoor area that hosts acts from Snoop Dogg to Willie Nelson.

SHOOTING STAR SALOON, HUNTSVILLE, UTAH

Whiskey Joe (who didn't get his name from drinking Mormon holy water) was once asked to leave, presumably for being a drunk bastard, and made a big shooting exit, aiming his bullets at the decorative star above the door. The Shooting Star is the oldest operating liquor-slinger in Utah, and has been sticking it to the Mormons since 1879.

OTP Tip: If you ever find yourself way up north in Tacoma, Washington, drop into coffeepot-shaped Bob's Java Jive for a beer, and only a beer, because they've got little else but kitsch on tap there.

NEVADA'S LOOSE SLOTS

Nevada is the state where your dollars turn to cents and your self-control ceases to exist. The state offers a range of ways to lose your money and your mind. While Vegas is by far the most popular place to temporarily live in sin, Nevada is also home to Reno and Laughlin, two cities with their own slightly scary versions of fun. From glam to sham, this is how you gamble away your dignity in the desert.

LAS VEGAS

When Las Vegas peeks out from the desert horizon and you finally convince yourself it's not a mirage (unless you're staying at the Mirage), the wonder of Sin City reveals itself one clamoring slot machine at a time. Nobody goes to Vegas to be tame; this desert oasis is overflowing with glamorous hedonism and the best thing to do is just give in to it. You come here to gamble with your money at the tables, your life at the buffets, and your morals at the clubs. The minute you step onto the strip, there will be a slot machine, blackjack table, or another contraption to suck your money out of your pockets in every direction.

A buffet will beckon you with its all-you-can-eat aromas coming out of every crevice of this place. The whole city runs on a twenty-four-hour clock, which means taking shots of tequila before noon is totally acceptable. You will be naked poolside, a stripper pole will find its way between your legs (maybe a real stripper will be up there, too), and you won't remember a thing once it's all said and done—until you check your bank account or your ring finger.

OTP Tip: If you don't quite make it to Vegas before getting the urge to throw it all down on red, you can hit Buffalo Bill's in Primm Valley, a second-rate Vegas-like hotel and casino that opened in 1994. Here, you can eat your weight in pancakes at Denny's, take a dip in the buffalo-shaped pool, and puke your guts out into the parking lot while riding the Desperado, a janky roller coaster that serpentines around the hotel.

RENO

Moving down the glam-gamble meter, Reno is the "Biggest Little City in the World," which is basically a load of crap. The entire town is like Weird Al Yankovic's party circus, curly mullet included. The casinos are old, the hotels are smelly, the drinks are sugary, and the whole place is run by what seems like carnival rejects. The upside is that everything is cheap and you can get the Awful Awful Burger at Rosie's Cafe in the Nugget Casino Resort in nearby Sparks, Nevada.

This thing is "awfully big, and awfully [debatably] good," with two 1/3 pound greasy-as-fuck patties, loaded with cheese and more grease, with a hint of vegetables and a Tabasco-y sauce on soggy buns. This burger is the poster boy for Reno, and once you're done Reno-reveling, you'll feel like joining a twelve-step program.

OTP Tip: Reno's location is great in that it's next door to Tahoe, where you can snowboard away any lingering aftertastes.

LAUGHLIN

A stretch of casino-dotted land along the Colorado River, Laughlin is the kind of place you regret visiting before even getting out of the car. First, there are sharps containers in every hotel bathroom for either (1) old diabetics or (2) heroin addicts; we haven't figured out which. Ninety-eight miles southeast of Vegas, Laughlin has a fat tourist riverboat feel, thanks to the Colorado Belle, a hotel built like a land-tied boat that goes absolutely nowhere. It's not quite Sin City and is more like a glorified arcade, but the river adds a little outdoor fun where you can ride your sads out on a Jet Ski.

The best eats are at chains like Bubba Gump's and Joe's Crab Shack, where you'll see obese families tackling crab legs. There are a few pools, weird shows, slots, and game tables, but, mostly, Laughlin is the kind of place you take someone you're not trying to impress very much. As the saying goes, "Whatever happens in Laughlin stays in Laughlin." Unless it's a case of the herp; take that shit to a hospital outside city lines pronto.

THE QUICK AND DIRTY ON BURNING MAN

Every year, people flock to Burning Man from all over the world and San Francisco empties and pours out its freaks into the dusty Nevada desert. Out in the middle of nowhere, a temporary community is created, where sharing is caring and clothes are always optional. For one week, thousands of people live together and mostly trip balls until they realize they'll have to wear shoes again come Monday. People start preparations for next year's Burning Man the minute they get back to civilization from the desert. It's a perpetual loop, a way of life for anybody who used to love building dioramas in elementary school. While the theme changes annually, here's what you can always expect at Burning Man.

GETTING STUCK IN SAND

En route to Burning Man, the excitement will always diminish for a while during the drive. You will pump yourself up with EDM and maybe start the revelry early in the car, but, inevitably, once you approach Black Rock, things will come to a screeching halt and the sandy dust from thousands of vehicles will invade your nostrils. These are the moments where you relinquish your city-dwelling cleanliness standards and embrace the fact that it's going to be a while before you have a proper shower.

DAY-GLO, GOGGLES, PONCHOS, ROLLERBLADES

There will always be a tricked-out bike, likely with drums attached, and footprint-free transportation around the Playa; Rollerblades or anything with wheels will give you a huge advantage in experiencing as many kooky installations as possible. Nudity, Day-Glo everythings, goggles, and ponchos are essential to weather the desert, and you'll find people bobbing around the desert wearing one or all of these things every year.

DIRTY MINDS, DIRTIER BODIES

While there will be lots of hooking up in random places, there won't be much by way of cleaning up the dirty spots on your body. You can count on someone coming through with some sort of group shower, but not one that'll actually de-funk anything.

One of the biggest principles of this make-shift community is to leave no trace behind. This means that soapy residue and runoff are prohibited. So prepare to leave a smell trail and nothing else behind.

GRAND SCALE SCULPTURE

While it changes with every year's new theme, people start working on their Burning Man art early in the year and in huge warehouses. Giant sculptures are transported to the burn in pieces and assembled on site. What they bring to the event will boggle your already mixed-up mind. Oh, and fire. There will always be fire.

THE UNEXPECTED

Whether it's some ridiculous idea, like a giant, climbable typewriter or the "Coney Island of the Mind" (a revival of carney posters), the art at Burning Man is always a surprising trip. You will travel from tent to tent and never encounter the same concept. From games to makeshift make-out bars, the deep desert of the Playa will always exceed even your wildest expectations. People like to play up their installations based on the assumption that you'll likely be doing psychedelics. Mir-rors, lights, and geometrical wonders will always be part of the design, and will feed your dilated pupils with mind candy (some-times real or drug-infused candy as well).

For Debbie Downers, Burning Man is the happiest week of the year in San Fran-cisco. You want to get ice cream at Bi-Rite during Saturday afternoon primetime ice cream hours? Or a morning bun at Tartine? The hourlong lines are cut down to nothing and San Francisco becomes a ghost town where you can frolic to your heart's con-tent until the Burners come back to bum everything out.

THE GREAT AMERICAN BEER FESTIVAL, DENVER, COLORADO

Americans may not know shit about Oktoberfest, but 'Merica can hold its own when it comes to beer, or at least have its own Septemberfest. America has nominated Colorado, which produces about 1.7 million barrels of craft beer annually, as the site for the frothy fun known as the Great American Beer Festival. Here's the breakdown on how Denver does the brew.

THE BEER

Every single beer you've ever tried (or dreamed of trying) is at this festival. Liked something you sipped in Portland? The fest hosts several handfuls of Portland breweries, including favorites like Deschutes and Fat Head's. San Francisco's 21st Amendment got your bubbles bubbling? It's here, along with so many others. In addition to breweries from Maine to Nebraska and everything in between, all of Colorado's hidden breweries come out of the mountains for the big event to showcase their hoppy bests.

NOBLE HOPS

The festival isn't just about getting your hands on a stein and your mouth around the best beer America has to offer; it's also a full-on competition between breweries from far and wide. The judging panel presides over ninety-two categories of beers for three days to determine which brews are deserving of the bronze, silver, and gold medals at stake. What do you get out of all this? The early bird news of which beers will be top sellers of the year, so you can impress your snobby beer-drinking friends with your abilities to suss out the duds from the sure-fire suds. The competition is private, but word of the winners makes it out to the public in no time.

PAIRED

Wine isn't the only drink that has food-pairing potential. While in college, beer (especially Guinness) may have doubled as breakfast, complementing this heady brew with bites is a more sophisticated approach to getting sloshed. Inside the Farm to Table Pavilion, James Beard Award–winning chefs gather to carefully prepare meals that pair perfectly with selected beers. For the poor man's approach, you can make a pretzel necklace with cheese sticks and Slim Jims in the main hall, and walk around pairing whateverthefuck you want with it.

THE SILENT DISCO

We're big proponents of finding the right balance between chugging beer and moving around so that it doesn't settle in the wrong places. The Silent Disco quietly brings down the house with a live DJ, sometimes inexplicably dressed like Elvis, pumping tunes into the headphones of willing participants. For out-loud music, the fest attracts bagpipers that spontaneously serenade the crowd throughout the day.

AROUND TOWN

If you didn't get your fill of beer at the fest, getting out into the fresh Denver air will put you face-to-face with some fantastic brew pubs (which often have food trucks at the ready). Our favorite is the heavy-metal taproom TRVE Brewing Co., where they add crazy shit to their beer (like smoked tea) and only charge you a buck for a three-ounce pour. Other local favorites are newcomers Jagged Mountain, Black Shirt Brewing Co. (look for the red door), and Great Divide Brewing Co., which continue to score medals from the Great American Beer Festival.

BEST PLACES TO SPEND THE HOLIDAYS

Most holidays in 'Merica are just an excuse to get wasted and fall deep into the one-burger-too-many food coma. While many people don't even know what most holidays are about, it's fun to celebrate in places that go all-out to honor St. Patrick, pull out traditional pilgrim shit for Thanksgiving, and take Halloween one step too far.

ST. PATRICK'S DAY, CHICAGO, ILLINOIS (MARCH)

No matter where you find yourself in 'Merica in the middle of March, chances are there will be a crowd of extremely drunk people wearing green and stumbling around the streets. Who was St. Patrick? Why are we wearing green? Doesn't matter. People who are actually Irish get king status for a night and Guinness is touted as the nectar of the gods. While there are many Irish enclaves around the country, the greenest spot to be on St. Patty's Day is along the river in Chicago. On St. Patty's Saturday, the river is dyed green and looks like a Ninja Turtle slime sewer. The surrounding area is engulfed by a parade that features all things Irish, including dancing, music, and cabbage.

MEMORIAL DAY, LAKE HAVASU, COLORADO (MAY)

On Memorial Day, Americans take advantage of the nice weather and hold intimate gatherings where the goal is to pass out before dinner. Raunch up your Memorial Day (it's really supposed to honor members of the armed forces who have sacrificed their lives to defend this country) at Lake Havasu, where bikinis only include the bottom part and boats are dangerously navigated by bros with the wheel in one hand and a beer in the other.

FOURTH OF JULY, WILLIAMSBURG, VIRGINIA (INDEPENDENCE DAY)

Aside from getting ceremoniously wasted, your goal on the Fourth is to get to a rooftop or a waterfront to watch the fireworks. The entire country is on the brink of blowing up on the Fourth, so why not celebrate in seventeenth-century glory? Get down with the first U.S. colony in colonial Williamsburg, Virginia, where, in addition to fireworks, muskets and cannons also go off to add to the drama. Prepare to get patriotic. It's only three hours from D.C., and if you can gather yourself on the fifth, you can go check out the Declaration of Independence, displayed at the National Archives Building.

LABOR DAY, SEATTLE, WASHINGTON (SEPTEMBER)

Labor Day will feel about the same as Memorial Day, just three months later. You should be celebrating the achievements of the American labor movement, but will use it as an excuse to get drunk outside before you need to wear pants again. The least labor-intensive place on Labor Day? Bumbershoot in Seattle, an art and music festival that'll send the summer off right. Bookend your summer with as much BBQ as you can swallow and pour a little beer out for the worker homies.

HALLOWEEN, SAN FRANCISCO, CALIFORNIA (OCTOBER)

People in SF dress up in drag throughout the year. If you peeked inside the closet of any San Franciscan, you'd find a one-to-one ratio of costumes to regular clothes (and likely more hoodies than you'd ever need anywhere else). You never know if you'll be called on to don a feather boa on a Monday night or a sparkly tutu on a Wednesday morning. Given all the glitzy regalia in San Franciscans' wardrobes, you'd best believe that Halloween in SF is a spectacle. The Halloween parade in the Castro is like a collage of the craziest things you'll ever see, with handcrafted costumes that outglitter the rest of the country.

THANKSGIVING, HOUSTON, TEXAS (NOVEMBER)

Thanksgiving is all about being grateful for what you've got; but if there isn't a massive, gluttonous feast in front of you come turkey day, getting a "thank-you" through your clenched jaw is going to be difficult. Sure, you can feast like a pilgrim in Plymouth, Massachusetts, complete with bonnets and people debunking traditional dishes and myths (which is annoying when all you're trying to do is see how many slices of pumpkin pie you can eat before vomiting). But we'd rather get our fill of tryptophan in Houston, where, in addition to the massive parade that goes down every Thanksgiving Day, many local restaurants hold prix fixe dinners and buffets with huge birds, massive steaks, and the kind of sides that'll clog your arteries the Texan way.

CHRISTMAS, SANTA CLAUS, INDIANA (DECEMBER)

Christmas is about family (or Jesus or something), lights, and presents. Cities all around the country decorate their streets with lights and pine trees to summon that elusive Christmas spirit we all want to feel every year. But while many cities can put on Christmas makeup, only one has committed to the holiday permanently. Santa Claus, Indiana, owns Christmas. In addition to a large, permanent statue of Santa Claus in the middle of town, this town's got Santa's Candy Castle and a post office that receives (and responds to) letters addressed to Santa. You can camp on Lake Rudolph and take Christmas Boulevard straight to Holiday World, a Santa-approved theme park and splashin' safari.

NEW YEAR'S, LAS VEGAS, NEVADA (JANUARY)

Watching the ball drop in Times Square means you'll have to hold onto your frozen piss for six hours in a crowd so tightly packed that expanding your lungs to breathe the frigid air becomes taxing. We think New Year's should be about making out—no more, no less (well, maybe champagne). So where is the best tongue action? Undoubtedly, Las Vegas. Casino club hopping and people's general wish to be as debaucherous as possible will put you in front of a lot of willing lips come midnight. Fireworks will be shot off every casino on the strip and stumbling into a stranger's arms is absolutely acceptable under the cover of Vegas's cliché motto. In the morning, you can start on your resolutions by the pool; that is, if you don't need to file for an annulment first.

ABOUT THE AUTHORS

FREDDIE PIKOVSKY

Freddie is the CEO of Off Track Planet and has his hands in every aspect of the company. He is the first U.S. born child of a family that emigrated from Ukraine forty years ago. Freddie grew up bicostal. He was born in Brooklyn, NY, then relocated to Los Angeles, CA, at a young age, and came back to Brooklyn where he created Off Track Planet in 2009. Recently, Freddie has spent time living in the Midwest and traveling around the country to explore parts of the United States less often seen.

ANNA STAROSTINETSKAYA

Anna is the Chief-of-Content at Off Track Planet and is the voice behind the brand. She was born in the former USSR and immigrated to Los Angeles in 1990. Anna studied abroad in Spain and moved to Brooklyn in 2009, where Off Track Planet was born. On a writing assignment, Anna left her heart in San Francisco and moved to the City by the Bay in 2015 to retrieve it. She now lives in the Mission District, eating veggie burritos and still trying to sell her NYC winter clothes.

ACKNOWLEDGMENTS

We'd like to thank the diverse group of Americans, emigrants, and American immigrants who have made this book possible. From greasy-spoon diner owners to middle-of-nowhere artists, risk-taking musicians, and daring fashionistas, this book is a tribute to the people who make America a wacky mishmash of traditions, cultures, and communities.

ANNA STAROSTINETSKAYA would like to thank her father, Alexander Starostinetksy, for having the courage to leave everything behind in order to bring her to this "land of opportunity." Her papa is the strongest, bravest, funniest man she knows.

FREDDIE PIKOVSKY would like to thank his parents for birthing him in Brooklyn, and Anna Homsey for dealing with him in Cincinnati and beyond.

PHOTO CREDITS

Front cover: Crux Creative/Creative Market.com; p. 3: Janet Hudson; p. 4 (top): Alexander Russy; p. 4 (bottom left): Jess Sloss; p. 4 (bottom right): Rich Anderson; pp. 5 (woman), 192 (right), 193 (top right): Parker Knight; pp. 5 (frozen fountain), 49, 66 (bottom left), 68: Anthony Quintano; pp. 5 (hot dog), 194 (left): Mike McCune; pp. 5 (house), 102 (bottom): Rona Proudfoot; p. 6 (left): Domenick D'Andrea; p. 6 (right): Henry P. Moore; p. 7 (map): Encyclopedia Americana, 1920; p. 7 (top right): A. J. Russell; p. 7 (center): Alexander Gardner; p. 7 (bottom): Vintage periods; p. 8 (top left): James Montgomery Flagg; pp. 8 (top right), 9 (top left): U.S. National Archives and Records Administration; p. 8 (bottom left): Sensei Alan; p. 9 (top right): NY World-Telegram, DeMarsico, Dick; p. 9 (bottom right): Shepard Fairey; pp. 13 (top left), 22, 23, 181 (bottom): Freddie Pikovsky; p. 13 (right), 42 (top and bottom): Eva Rinaldi; pp. 13 (bottom left), 17: Rick Audet/Richard Audet; p. 14: Nicholas A. Tonelli; p. 15 (top): Ron B; p. 15 (bottom): Richard "rxb"; p. 16 (top): "patchattack"; p. 16 (bottom): Miguel Vieira; p. 18: Jason Rasp; p. 19 (Derby/top): Bill Brine; p. 19 (horse hat/top left): ScubaBear68; p. 19 (mint juleps/middle): Jeremy T. Hetzel; p. 19 (hats/bottom): Lee Burchfield; p. 20 (Dale Earnhardt/top): Darryl Moran; p. 20 (middle): Ryan Dickey; p. 20 (Richard Petty/bottom): Ted Van Pelt; p. 20 (racing flags): Ryan Burke/Thinkstock; p. 21 (top left): "o_dmentd_o"; p. 21 (top right): "PSParrot"; p. 21 (bottom right): U.S. Army; p. 24 (top): Randy Heinitz; p. 24 (bottom): Jo Naylor; p. 25: Don Heaton; pp. 26, 215 (right): Ed Uthman; p. 27 (left): Chris M. Morris; pp. 27 (right), 46 (bottom): "Prayitno"; pp. 28, 29 (bottom), 61 (top): "BobIsTraveling"; p. 29 (top): Government & Heritage Library, State Library of NC; pp. 30 (top), 31, 85 (Pho Junkies/bottom): Elvert Barnes; p. 30 (bottom): Michael Fleshman; p. 32 (left): "Long Horn Dave"; p. 32 (right): Chauncey Davis; p. 33: Nancy Nance; pp. 34, 53: Emilio Labrador; p. 35: "Lwp Kommunikáció"; pp. 36 (bottom left), 41, 98 (left): Southern Foodways Alliance; p. 36 (top right): Kent Wang; p. 36 (bottom right): George Kelly; pp. 37, 117 (top left), 155 (bottom): Arnold Gatilao; p. 38: "joyosity"; p. 39 (top): Tam Warner Minton; p. 39 (bottom): Chris Gent; p. 40: David Hunkins; p. 42 (middle): Avarty Photos; p. 43 (top left): Shannon McGee; p. 43 (top right): Curtis Fockele; p. 43 (bottom right): Joe Van; p. 44 (top): United States Library of Congress; p. 44 (bottom right): Josh Czupryk; p. 45: "Anonymous Account"; p. 46 (top): Casey and Sonja; pp. 47 (top), 206 (right): Cliff "cliff1066"; p. 47 (bottom): "countryboy1949"; p. 48 (Elvis/top): Kevin Dooley; p. 48 (Graceland House/top middle): Lindsey Turner; p. 48 (Elvis grave/bottom middle): Mark Gstohl; p. 48 (Elvis statue/bottom): Kathleen Conklin; pp. 51 (top), 52 (right): Neon Tommy; p. 51 (bottom): "slgckgc"; p. 52 (left): Texas A&M University; p. 54 (left): MarkScottAustinTX; p. 54 (right): "hans_castorp2010"; p. 57 (top left): Elliott P.; p. 57 (top right): Daniel Rosenstein; p. 57 (bottom): Lokesh Dhakar; p. 58 (left): Daniel D'Auria; p. 58 (right): Jackie "Sister72"; p. 58 (bottom): Boston Public Library; p. 59: Roman Iakoubtchik; p. 60: Joseph Bylund; p. 61 (middle): "dwstucke"; p. 61 (bottom): Alex "eflon"; p. 62 (top): Richard Schatzberger; p. 62 (bottom): Patrick "pdbreen"; p. 63: Mike "StillWellMike"; pp. 64, 65 (top): Boris Dzhingarov; p. 65 (middle): Stacey Gitto; pp. 65 (bottom), 107 (top): Doug Kerr; p. 66 (top right): Ralph Hockens; p. 67 (top): Kevin Burkett; p. 67 (bottom): Kenny Louie; p. 69 (top): Michael Moore for the Pacific Pinball Museum; p. 69 (bottom): Roger LeJeune; p. 70: David Shankbone; p. 71: Dave Michuda; p. 72: Jonas Strandell; p. 72 (swallow tattoo): Anton Senkou-Melnick/Thinkstock; p. 73 (top right): Tom Bastin; p. 73 (bottom left): "pshutterbug"; p. 74: Eric Brumble; p. 75 (top): "6SN7"; p. 75 (bottom): Alexis Lamster; p. 76 (left): Pedro Cambra; p. 76 (right): "dumbonyc"; p. 77 (left): Vlastimil Koutecký; p. 77 (right): Tekniska Museet; p. 78: Georg Petschnigg; p. 79: "Fashionby He"; p. 80: Caboose Spice & Company; p. 81: Ginny "ginnerobot"; p. 82: Joe Hall; p. 83 (top): La Piazza Pizzeria; p. 83 (bottom): The Pizza Review; p. 84 (top): Jane "janezorz"; pp. 84 (bottom), 85 (food trucks/top), (red food truck/bottom): Ted Eytan; pp. 86, 140 (right): Bernt Rostad; p. 87 (left): Mandy "amanderson2"; p. 87 (right): "_e.t"; pp. 88, 89 (middle and bottom): The All-Nite Images; p. 89 (top): "Eden, Janine, and Jim"; p. 90: Ric Manning; p. 91: "Omasz"; pp. 92, 93 (left): Dig Boston; p. 93 (right): Richard Howe; pp. 94, 95: "istolethetv"; p. 96: Connie Ma; p. 97 (top): Matthew Bellemare; p. 97 (bottom): Caroline Culler; p. 98 (right): Alyson Hurt; p. 101 (top left): Andy McLemore; p. 101 (bottom left): Jona Park; p. 101 (right): Steve Jurvetson; p. 102 (top): Jolene "Jolene4ever"; p. 102 (middle): Harris Walker; p. 103: Artur

Staszewski; p. 104: Thomas Crenshaw; p. 105 (top): Terry Alexander; p. 105 (top middle): "John5199"; p. 105 (bottom middle): "b0jangles"; p. 105 (bottom): Anna Fox; pp. 106 (left), 127: Derek Jensen "tysto"; p. 106 (right): Andrew Keith; p. 107 (bottom): Megan Scanlin; p. 108: Jeremy Thompson; p. 109 (top): "Coasterman1234"; p. 109 (bottom): Dusso Janladde; p. 110: "Jim, the Photographer"; p. 111: Jason Taellious; p. 112 (top): New York World-Telegram & Sun Newspaper Photograph Collection; pp. 112 (bottom), 183 (top): James Vaughan; p. 113: Pablo Sanchez; p. 114: Dave S "That Hartford Guy"; p. 115 (top): Museum at FIT; p. 115 (middle): The Coincidental Dandy; p. 115 (bottom): Achim Hepp; p. 116 (top): "A Gude"; p. 116 (bottom): "regan76"; p. 117 (bottom right): Edsel Little; p. 118 (left): photog diane; p. 118 (right): Muu-karhu; p. 119 (left): Steve Moses; p. 119 (right): "m01229"; p. 120: Phil Roeder; p. 121 (left): "Loozrboy"; p. 121 (right): "buba69"; p. 122 (top): Angela George; pp. 122 (middle), 123 (left): Motown Records; p. 122 (bottom): Arnie Lee; p. 123 (right): CBS Television; p. 124 (left): "Music54"; p. 124 (right): Jason H. Smith; p. 125 (left): "Ryanw2313"; p. 125 (top right): Seher Sikandar; p. 125 (bottom right): Judy Glova; p. 126: The Zender Agenda; pp. 128, 129 (top): James Carr; p. 129 (bottom): Ben Jacobson; p. 130 (top): Nate Bolt; p. 130 (bottom): "switz1873"; p. 131: U.S. Air Force; p. 132 (left): Frank Pierson; p. 132 (right): "Skudrafan1"; pp. 135 (left), 166 (bottom left and right), 167: J.T (Jason) Thorne; p. 135 (right): Kurt Magoon; p. 136: Nan Palmero; p. 137 (left): Zachary Collier; p. 137 (right): Cecil Sanders; p. 138 (top): Joseph Sparks; p. 138 (bottom): "AllAroundTheWest"; p. 139 (top): Kaila Angello; pp. 139 (bottom), 202, 206 (left): David Fulmer; pp. 140 (left), 174 (top and bottom): "InSapphoWeTrust"; p. 141 (top): Bryan Ungard; p. 141 (middle): Yellowstone National Park; p.141 (bottom): Dino Trnjanin; p. 142: Rise Studio; p. 143: Aaron Vowels; p. 144 (top): Wayne Porter; p. 144 (bottom): "Mariersal4"; p. 145: Eli Duke; p. 146: "Daderot"; p. 147 (left and bottom right): Ansgar Walk; p. 147 (top right): Alfred Cook; p. 148: Kyle Rush; p. 149 (top): Christopher Michel; pp. 149 (bottom left), 156 (top): Mike Mozart; p. 149 (bottom right): Robert Lawton; p. 150 (left): Julie Gomoll; p. 150 (right): Chris Lott; p. 151 (top): Bill & Vicki T; p. 151 (bottom): "Renee"; p. 152: Tim Evanson; p. 153: "adrigu"; p. 154 (top): Joe Haupt; p. 154 (bottom): "SenseiAlan"; p. 155 (top): Lenin and McCarthy; p. 156 (bottom): Matthew W. Jackson; p.157 (top): "rayb777"; pp. 157 (bottom), 158 (right): Jonathunder; p. 158 (left): Stephen Mihalcik; p. 159 (top): miss eskimo-la-la; p. 159 (middle): Bradley P Johnson; p. 159 (bottom): Yutaka Seki; p. 160: Daniel Farrell; p. 161: Eugene Kim; p. 162 (left): Joe Mabel; p. 162 (right): "Dori"; p. 163: Cynthia Frankenburg; p. 164: Maha Music Festival; p. 166 (top): Chris Heald; pp. 168, 169: Larry Jacobsen; p. 171 (left): Michael Fraley; p. 171 (right): Jeff Gunn; p. 172: Heather Cowper; p. 173 (top): "Frank_am_Main"; p. 173 (bottom): Mike Vondran; p. 174 (middle): Lin Mei; p. 175 (top): Kelly "KellyK"; p. 175 (top middle, bottom middle, bottom): Forsaken Fotos; p. 176: Ronnie Macdonald; p. 177: Grand Canyon National Park; p. 178 (top): Matt Turner; p. 178 (bottom): John Fowler; p. 179 (top): "McD22"; p. 179 (middle): Oregon Department of Transportation; p. 179 (bottom): "tq2cute"; p. 180 (left): "SarahTz"; p. 180 (right): Karen Blaha; p. 181 (top): Madeleine Deaton; p. 182: ADTeasdale; p. 183 (bottom): Jessica Rossi; p. 184 (top): Connie "conbon33"; p.184 (bottom): Melodie Turori; p. 185 (left): Andrij Bulba; p. 185 (right): Quinn Dombrowski; p. 186: "cobalt123"; p. 187 (top): Woody Hibbard; p. 187 (bottom): Don Graham; p. 188 (top): Ryan Basilio; p. 188 (bottom): Alonzo "LosAnheles"; p. 189 (top left): Ryan Vaarsi; p. 189 (top right and bottom left): Omar Laribi; p. 189 (bottom right): "doktajones"; p. 190 (left): Rojer; p. 190 (right): Fred Rockwood; p. 191: Brad Spry; p. 192 (left): Danny Casillas; p. 193 (top left): Louie Baur; p. 193 (bottom): "p-a-t-r-i-c-k"; p. 194 (right): Meg Rutherford; p. 195 (top): Francis Storr; p. 195 (bottom): "Szapucki"; p. 196 (top): Herb Neufeld; p. 196 (bottom): Navin Rajagopalan; p. 197 (top): T.Tseng; p. 197 (bottom): Kyle Van Horn; p. 198: Cord Rodefeld; p. 199 (top): Jeremy Keith; p. 199 (bottom): "GoToVan"; p. 200: Calgary Reviews; p. 201 (left): Samson Loo; p. 201 (right): Ed Schipul; p. 203: "Themom51"; p. 204 (left): Leif Maxfield; p. 204 (right): David Lee; p. 205 (left): Reno Tahoe Territory; p. 205 (right): Sarah Nichols; p. 207 (left): Nick Ares; p. 207 (right): Bill Mulder; p. 208 (left): Matthew Straubmuller; p. 208 (right): Anna Irene; p. 209 (bottom left): Sharon Rong; p. 209 (top right): Daniel Ramirez; p. 209 (bottom right): Arturo Sotillo; p. 210 (left): Hawaii Savvy; p. 210 (right): Fabrice Florin; p. 211 (top): Jennifer Morrow; p. 211 (middle): Ian Norman; p. 211 (bottom): Cory Doctorow; pp. 212, 213: Daniel Spiess; p. 214: Max Talbot-Minkin; p. 215 (left): Kevin Prichard

INDEX